K

FOLK
TALES

KERRY

FOLK TALES

GARY BRANIGAN AND LUKE EASTWOOD

The
History
Press
Ireland

First published 2019

The History Press
97 St George's Place
Cheltenham
GL50 3QB
www.thehistorypress.co.uk

British Library Cataloguing in Publication Data.
A catalogue record for this book is available from the British Library.

ISBN 978 0 7509 8414 0

Typesetting and origination by The History Press
Printed and bound by TJ International Ltd

*Dedicated to my ancestors, the Scannells and Ó Scanaills of
Castleisland and Tralee* – Gary

*Dedicated to Elena Danaan, who has supported and encouraged
all of my writings, including this work* – Luke

CONTENTS

ACKNOWLEDGEMENTS

We would like to express our sincere gratitude to many people for the kind assistance, guidance and encouragement received, both directly and indirectly, during the compilation of this publication.

Research Facilities at the National Library of Ireland, Kerry County Museum, Dingle Library, National Museum of Ireland (Country Life), Royal Society of Antiquaries of Ireland, Office of Public Works, Ordnance Survey Ireland, UCD, and the various local historical, folkloric, and heritage societies have all been invaluable, and thanks go to the wonderful staff who maintain them.

Special mentions deserve to go to Críostóir Mac Cárthaigh of the National Folklore Collection at UCD; to Nicola Guy of The History Press for her endless patience and ongoing assistance during the publication process; and to Elena Danaan: artist, book illustrator, jewellery and fabric designer, and all round good person, who created the absolutely amazing images for the book and to whom we owe a significant debt of gratitude. I would urge everybody to check out her fantastic website at www.elenadanaan.com.

Thanks also to the others, too many to mention here, who assisted in various ways in bringing this book to completion.

I am deeply grateful to Gary Branigan for kindly asking me to assist him in the writing of this book. After almost twenty years of living in County Wexford, I arrived in Dingle as a blow-in with no great ties to the town or County Kerry generally. This was a very unexpected and somewhat daunting opportunity. Despite my fears, it has been a great honour and pleasure to research, uncover and retell these Kerry stories, many of which had fallen into obscurity. I'm also profoundly grateful to Elena Danaan (who illustrated this book) and my friends and family who have supported and encouraged my writing, including this work.

Luke Eastwood
Dingle / Daingean Uí Chúis
January 2019

Without the great help of my co-author Luke Eastwood and illustrator Elena Danaan this book would simply not have been possible, and I extend my sincere thanks to them both. Throughout this challenging journey, Jeannette, Tara, Aoife and Rory have been there, providing an un-ending supply of love, support, encouragement and patience. Words alone cannot express my sincere gratitude and appreciation to them for everything.

Gary Branigan
Dingle / Daingean Uí Chúis
January 2019

INTRODUCTION

So much has been written of the rich indigenous culture extant in our fair isle. From language and customs to dress, music and folklore, the island peoples on the western fringes of Europe are celebrated for their unique way of life.

Within Ireland, many localities have their own idiosyncrasies and home-grown traditions, stories and lore borne out of local history and local circumstance. The kingdom of Kerry is no exception, and this book was created with the intention of sharing and celebrating some of its wealth of local tales and folklore.

Many of these stories are old and have been handed down from generation to generation by local people for local people, while others are more modern, showing the continuance of the Irish traditions of the seanachaí and of Irish storytelling. In reading through the various tales gathered here, the reader will be transported to a time and place long gone, but forever preserved.

Our contribution to this collection of folk tales is in our capacity as storytellers, and in the most part not as academics or historians. Fact and fable, however, are inextricably woven into the fabric of the Irish gene and it is not always possible to separate them, but we have attempted to be as faithful as we can to both.

The medium of telling stories and singing songs is the way the Irish have been able to come to terms with fortune and misfortune alike. It is our hope and belief that anybody will be able to pick up this book and easily enjoy the rich bounty of Kerry's storytelling tradition.

In selecting tales for inclusion in this publication, we have tried our best to cover from a range generally representative of the county as a whole. Kerry, affectionately known as 'The Kingdom' is the fifth largest county on the island and one of the six that form the province of Munster. Named after the peoples of Ciarraige who inhabited this ancient territory, Kerry possesses an unparalleled tapestry of history and folklore, and is central to many of Ireland's most famous and fantastic myths and legends.

1

History

Black '47

There have been far too many bad times in Ireland over the millennia. Our history is spattered with an untold number of stories of grief and suffering.

One such distressing time was nearly 170 years ago, when the vicious blight travelled over on the warm air from Europe and infected the valuable potatoes growing in the ground, causing them to turn black and rot. Such was the scourge of the affliction that there were twice as many people living in Ireland then as there are now, with many departing this life or this land for places better – God be good to them.

The people all over the island had only small plots of land that they rented from the English landlords, and it was from these wee plots that they eked out an existence for themselves and their families. The only thing they had to grow and eat were lumper potatoes and the disease ravaged the lumper the worst of all, leaving people with nothing to eat, practically overnight.

The poor people grew weak and became desperate. Those that survived the first year tried to sow the rotten seed potatoes the following season in the hope of getting a crop, but nothing grew. Many then did the unthinkable and butchered their donkeys and dogs for food in the hope that this blight would pass, but it did not. It wasn't long before the people started to die of starvation, and the heavy odour of rotten spuds and death settled over the land. People were dying so quickly that they could not make the coffins fast enough, and there are even accounts of people being buried alive.

There is one particular story from Kerry of a man who was being placed into a grave, when he awoke saying, 'Do not bury me for I am not yet dead.' The doctor at the graveside, who had lost his mind through sheer exhaustion, said, 'You are a liar! The doctor knows best!' and the trench was filled in.

The blight started to take hold in 1845 and grew in strength and severity until the height of 1847, when land and communities were decimated. This year was so bad that it became known as Black '47. Many people had to leave their houses in the mornings and go around from place to place, looking for something, anything, to eat. Many even ate grass in the hope of getting some sustenance but, of course, it was of little benefit.

When all other options were exhausted, they could apply to be taken into one of the union workhouses in Listowel, Tralee, Dingle, Killarney, Cahersiveen, or Kenmare. These workhouses were set up to look after those who could not look after themselves, and many were horrid but necessary places, full of desperate people in desperate situations. It is true that starvation subsided for many in the workhouses, as they received meager rations of financial aid and yellow meal, but painful deaths continued at the same levels as before from fever, dysentery, and scurvy.

As the famine intensified, workhouses became so overcrowded and underfunded that they began turning people away, resulting in the destitute being left to die at the roadsides and in the ditches.

Elena Danaan

After burying his sister without a priest, Myles Foley had reached breaking point. His poor sister had been turned away from the local workhouse in Tralee just the day before, and the cold November weather outside proved too much for her already frail body. In equal measures of anger and grief, he strung a black burial shroud across a large stick taken from a tree and painted the words 'Flag of Distress' on it. Then he gathered the support of his remaining family and neighbours and they marched in formation to the workhouse, demanding that they be allowed entry or would force their way in. The superintendent and other officers locked the gate and barricaded the door with furniture, but desperation led to the men and women pulling the gate off its hinges and pushing their way in through the door.

As they got inside the main entrance hall, they found that waiting for them were several members of the local constabulary, armed with batons. The guards did not hesitate in beating the poor wretches mercilessly, forcing them back out on to the road. Two of the men had received such a hiding that they died right there. There was no charity for those in need of charity in those times and, sadly, this is just one of many such stories of how philanthropy and oppression went hand in hand at that dark time in our history.

THE BURNING OF BALLYLONGFORD

We shall begin by quoting the famous playwright, novelist and poet, Oscar Wilde, who said: 'we are all in the gutter, but some of us are looking at the stars.' This, for us, demonstrates the feelings of the downtrodden people of Ireland in the early part of the last century.

Not long ago our fair isle celebrated the centenary of the great rebellion, which kick-started a chain of events leading to the independence of the majority of the Irish people.

Kerry is unfortunately noted as being the county to suffer the Rising's first tragic death, which occurred at Ballykissane Pier just outside the town of Killorglin. Although the rebellion was initially a failure, it caused such a stirring within the Irish people that the flame that ignited inside them has never been quenched.

Following these events, unrest grew fast in Ireland and the British government responded by setting up and dispatching a new battalion of soldiers made up of ex-servicemen and ex-convicts. In reality these soldiers, who came to be known as the Black and Tans, were no more than ruffians and thugs. While the Black and Tans were given a free hand to torment and rampage their way throughout the island at will, young Irishmen and Irishwomen came together and organised themselves into independent militias known as 'flying columns'. Their aim was to protect their communities against these men and show that they were no longer willing to lie down.

Members of these flying columns ended up on a wanted list, with many left with no option but to leave their families and go on the run. One such man, Eddie Carmody of Sallowglen, was ambushed on the road outside Ballylongford in the winter of 1920. Such was the cruelty of the Tans that they seized the poor unarmed man on the road and shot him several times at close range. He survived, however, and was able to crawl away and stay hidden from them for a while. The Tans frantically looked for him to finish the job and followed the drops of blood left by him on the road. They found him slumped against a ditch and, showing no mercy, dragged him back into the middle of the road and took turns to beat him with rifle butts. Only when they had inflicted enough suffering on the poor man did they finish him off by stabbing him several times.

If this were not enough, they then put his lifeless body on the back of an open cart and displayed it throughout the town, dumping it outside the barracks and leaving it there overnight before allowing his father to collect his body the next day.

This heinous and unnecessary act did not go unnoticed, and the local column made plans and bided their time. In the following spring, in reprisal for the vicious murder of Carmody, two Black and Tan men were shot dead while walking on the Well Road in the town of Ballylongford. This happened in the evening and word of what had happened spread fast throughout the town. Fearing revenge, people stayed indoors and quenched any candles or lanterns in the hope that they would not draw any attention to themselves. When reports of the murders reached the barracks, the remaining officers set upon the local populace with rampant vigour and, with the stench of alcohol on their breaths, set fire to furze bushes and pushed them in through smashed windows and onto the roofs of several cottages and houses in the area.

Elena Danaan

Any person who met them while they were in their destructive rage did not survive to tell the tale. In typical fashion, the Tans did not concern themselves with the possibility that there could be anybody inside any of the buildings, or indeed with the actual loss of property.

The fires were helped by the fact that the majority of houses were thatched and the weather was unusually dry for that time of the year. The resulting inferno spread quickly across the rooftops, destroying Well Street and Main Street in their entirety, with other areas also affected. Nothing but charred rubble, ashes, and waking nightmares were left behind.

THE ROSE OF TRALEE

The Rose of Tralee festival has become famous all over the world, especially among the Irish diaspora. It was begun by a group of local businessmen in 1957, who resurrected the former Race Week Carnival in an effort to attract more tourism to the town. The festival soon found success, with it being rebranded as the Rose of Tralee in 1959 to capitalise on the well-known nineteenth-century love song of the same name and adopting the festival format that we know today. This decision saw the festival transform from a local gathering into an international event.

At the outset, it was a small affair held on a small scale with a corresponding small budget, and only featuring women from Tralee, but by the early 1960s it was extended to include any women from Kerry, and finally in 1967 to include all women of Irish ancestry.

The song, attributed to poet Edward Mordaunt Spencer and violinist Charles William Glover, was published in the 1850s. It is based on actual historical events experienced by the writer William Mulchinock, and the loss of his love, Mary O'Connor. There is no doubt that their tragic story has left an enduring legacy for the town of Tralee, making it famous the world over.

William Pembroke Mulchinock was born in Tralee around 1820 to wealthy Protestant parents, who were prominent in the wool and linen trade. The family all lived happily at West Villa in nearby Ballyard until the premature deaths of both the father and young brother in close proximity to each other. William, who was reputedly a lay about, dreamer and poet, was particularly devastated by his brother's death and consoled himself with the usual pastimes of any young man of means. It was on one such outing, at the fair of Ballinasloe, that William met and instantly fell in love with a young lady by the name of Alice Keogh.

On returning to Tralee, he visited his sister Maria and his two young nieces, Anna and Margaret. It was here that he met the children's maid for the first time, another young lady by the name of Mary O'Connor. She was a great beauty with lustrous long dark hair, captivating eyes, pale skin and remarkable grace. Some might think that William was fickle, but whether he was or was not is a different story. As soon as he laid eyes on Mary, he was immediately lovestruck and forgot all about Alice, his former love.

It is believed that Mary was also born in or around 1820 to her dairymaid mother and shoemaker father. They all lived together in a small house on the aptly named Brogue Maker's Lane. Her mother was employed by John Mulchinock at his Cloghers House residence, which in turn enabled the young Mary to find work as a kitchen maid at West Villa for the Mulchinocks. Having proven to be intelligent and reliable, Mary was chosen by William's sister Maria as maid to her two children, which led to her finally meeting William.

On the pretext of visiting his nieces, William took every opportunity to visit Mary. In no time at all, the young couple fell madly in love and despite the disapproval of his family, they began courting and were engaged within a few weeks.

In the very different Ireland of the time, the engagement of an upper-class Anglo-Irish Protestant to a Catholic servant scandalised both families and local society. William's political leanings concerned many, and his involvement with Young Ireland and the Repeal Association infuriated his loyalist relatives and only served to create enemies for himself. The day following their engagement, William attended a Daniel

O'Connell political meeting in Denny Street. There, he unintentionally became embroiled in an altercation, whereby one of his companions instigated a fight with a gentleman by the name of Leggett and seriously wounded him with a sword. Although William intervened to end the conflict, a dragoon captain at the scene held William responsible for the incident and warned him that he would be arrested if the man died.

Shortly afterwards, and while William was spending some time with Mary, his best friend Robert Blennerhassett appeared on the scene with the terrible news that Leggett had died of his wounds, and what should have been a joyous occasion with his new fiancée became one of great sorrow as the two lovers were torn apart.

Blennerhassett insisted that William leave the country as quickly as possible and assisted him in doing so, but before leaving he promised Mary that he would return to her as soon as it was safe to do so.

William eventually settled in India and found himself working as a correspondent on the North-West Frontier. Having conducted himself well, the military authorities in India intervened on his behalf, obtaining Dublin Castle's permission for him to return home to Ireland in 1849.

William returned to Tralee from his long exile and stayed at the Kings Arms in the Rock, close by where Mary's family lived. He could not contain his excitement at the thought of their reunion, but just as he stepped outside his lodgings with the intention to visit her, a large funeral procession passed him on the street. Asking his landlord who the poor unfortunate to be buried was, his heart sank in horror when he heard that it was a local unmarried woman named Mary O'Connor, who had died of consumption in the poorhouse at just 29 years old. The poor man was heartbroken and often visited her grave at Clogherbrien cemetery, but without his sweetheart and with

Ireland still suffering from the ravages of the famine, there was little incentive for him to stay. He emigrated to America and married, seemingly to his former love Alice Keogh, and they had two children.

William's collection of 'Ballads and Songs' was published in New York in 1851, but this did not feature any mention of his Rose. Although he tried, William Mulchinock never fully recovered from the heartbreaking loss of Mary and after a few years his marriage failed and he returned to Tralee. In his pining for Mary he suffered from depression and alcoholism, and died at his home in Nelson Street in 1864, at 44 years of age.

SMALL BUT MIGHTY: THE VILLAGE OF LIXNAW

Lixnaw, in the north of the county, has been described as an insignificant village in current times, but it was once a thriving and important place – and not to mention the seat of the great Fitzmaurice clan, Barons of Kerry, since the early thirteenth century. During the time of Nicholas, 3rd Baron Kerry, a great number of improvements had been made to the local infrastructure, including the once proud castle, the bridge over the River Brick, and many other contributions to the small town and its environs, which improved the lot of the locals.

Another dominant era in Lixnaw was during the Nine Years' War, when the town once again became a central place in regional and national affairs, being, as it was, a front in that war. The conflict was instigated by Hugh O'Neill, then fought between Thomas Fitzmaurice, 18th Baron Kerry, and the English forces in a bloody engagement.

It all began in the summer of 1600 when Sir Charles Wilmot, who would later become Viscount Wilmot of

Athlone, took command of English forces and stormed the town, much to the great shame and dismay of the Fitzmaurices, who had undermined the castle in preparation for its demolition. Wilmot's surprise attack enabled him to take the castle, where he quickly established a garrison and made it his centre of operations. Thomas Fitzmaurice should have inherited the Earldom, castle and lands at Lixnaw following the death of his father Patrick in Dublin Castle but these were forfeit as a punishment for their rebellion.

Compounding the Fitzmaurice's losses, the following month Wilmot gleefully seized another one of their fortresses, Listowel Castle, after a siege of just sixteen days.

Two years later, Fitzmaurice was successful in re-taking his hereditary seat at Lixnaw, expelling the English garrison and leaving his brother Gerald in command. However, it was to be a short-lived success, and in an episode of military ping-pong Wilmot again seized it by swimming his men and horses across the moat and laying siege to the stronghold once more.

Thomas Fitzmaurice, now a fugitive stripped of his lands and any hope of a pardon, evaded further attempts to capture him and fought on in reduced circumstances as the war continued into 1603. Amazingly, after the death of Elizabeth I and the ascension of James I, Thomas succeeded in gaining a pardon from the new king and even obtained the re-grant of the title and lands of his father Patrick.

His descendants continued as Barons of Kerry, becoming Earls of Kerry from 1723 onwards, including William Petty-Fitzmaurice (Earl of Kerry, Marquess of Lansdowne and Earl of Shelburne). William, who grew up in Lixnaw, went on to become prime minister of England in 1782.

Today, nothing at Lixnaw remains of the once illustrious seat of the Kerry earls.

THE SIEGE OF SMERWICK AND THE DOWNFALL OF THE GERALDINES

The Fitzgeralds or Geraldines, Earls of Desmond, and the Butlers, Earls of Ormonde, were two of the most powerful families in Ireland since the Norman invasion; they maintained an intense rivalry down through the centuries that sometimes spilled over into bloody warfare. This bitter feud was effectively ended by the second Desmond rebellion and the subsequent demise of the Geraldine dynasty, but the conclusion did not happen overnight.

Following the first Desmond rebellion, led by James Fitzmaurice Fitzgerald, Fitzmaurice was pardoned but stripped of his lands as punishment. His cousin, the earl, also evicted him from rented land, leaving him effectively in poverty.

In 1575, Fitzmaurice fled to France and began seeking the assistance of Catholic powers in Europe, eventually making his way to Rome to petition Pope Gregory XIII for help. After securing modest assistance, an abortive invasion occurred in 1578 that subsequently led him to return to Rome, seeking further support.

The following year he departed from Spain with a small force of Spanish, Italian and Irish troops, and made his way via the English Channel. He captured two English vessels en route, before arriving at Dingle Harbour in mid July.

On 18 July 1579, the party relocated to Smerwick Harbour at Ard na Caithne, further west on the same peninsula. Here they took advantage of a long disused Iron-Age fort, Dún An Oír (fortress of gold), to establish their garrison, creating new earthworks on the promontory.

With the assistance of papal commissary Nicholas Saunders, Fitzmaurice declared a holy war on Elizabeth I at Dingle with much ceremony, calling upon Ireland to rise up against the heretic queen, who had been excommunicated in 1570.

Fitzmaurice's forces numbered roughly 100 men, and although two more Spanish galleys arrived soon after with a further 100 troops, it is clear that without raising support his rebellion would have been easily crushed.

Irked by the English authorities undermining Desmond's power, John of Desmond and his brother James entered the fray on 1 August with the assassination of two English officials in Tralee. Having secured some support from relatives, Fitzmaurice himself was only to play a small role in the war and, having travelled north into the province of Connacht to raise further support, he was killed in a skirmish with the Burkes after his men foolishly stole some horses from his cousin Theobald Burke.

The rebellion was now well underway and leadership was left to John of Desmond, who took over much of south Munster, raising some 2,000 men. In response, the English Lord Deputy brought 600 troops to Limerick, joining forces with Sir Nicholas Malby, Lord President of Connacht, and his army of over a thousand.

Up until now the Earl of Desmond, Gerald Fitzgerald, had stayed out of the conflict and had even given up his son as a hostage to guarantee his loyalty, but strictly on the condition that his lands not be attacked. After the plundering of Geraldine territory and the demand that the earl hand over his castle, the situation changed. Gerald refused to leave Askeaton Castle and, despite assurances from the English, he was declared a traitor, which left him with no choice but to enter the war on the side of the rebels. In November of that year he sacked Youghal in County Cork, escalating the conflict to all-out war and imploring Irish lords to defend Ireland and its Catholic faith.

In July 1580, following the rising of the O'Byrnes in Wicklow, the English sent a new army of 6,000 men under the new Lord Deputy, Baron Arthur Grey. After an initial humiliating defeat at Glenmalure, Grey marched his men south into

Munster to support the English forces there, unleashing a campaign of terror that would be long remembered.

Pope Gregory, whose hand was stoking the fires of war across Europe, intervened once again in Ireland. Having failed to convince Philip II of Spain, who had his own difficulties with the Dutch and Ottomans, to invade Ireland, the Pope secured ships to transport a force of around 700 Spanish, Italian and Basque troops under the command of Sebastiano di San Giuseppe.

The Papal army arrived in Smerwick Harbour on 10 September 1580, joining the small force at Dún An Oír before heading inland to join the Earl of Desmond, John Desmond and Lord Baltinglass. However, the English had somehow gained knowledge of the invasion and, with a force of around 4,000 men, Lord Grey and the Earl of Ormonde marched to cut them off.

Meanwhile, a naval blockade provided by Sir Richard Bingham prevented them leaving by sea to join the Irish rebels elsewhere. Trapped in the Dingle peninsula, Giuseppe was forced to retreat to Smerwick and make what they could of the defenses at Dún An Oír.

In October, Grey took his forces as far as Dingle and waited for supplies and eight cannons to arrive by sea with Admiral Winter at Smerwick. With the Papal forces trapped by the English on one side, the sea behind them and Mount Brandon on the other, Grey was in no hurry. When the artillery finally arrived on 5 November, preparations began for the siege, which started two days later.

Hopelessly outnumbered and remorselessly pounded by three warships in the harbour and many artillery pieces on land, the rebels stood little chance in a fort consisting mainly of earthworks. Despite this, they held out for three full days, although Giuseppe rather cowardly tried to bargain with Grey by releasing three local allies to the English. The three men, including a priest (Fr Laurence Moore) were horrifically tortured to no avail, before being used for target practice as the siege continued.

Finally, on 10 November, the defenders could take no more and surrendered to Grey's terms, which were apparently that they would be spared. However, Grey, in his report to Elizabeth I, maintained that he had demanded an unconditional surrender and 'that they should render the fort to me and yield their selves to my will for life or death'.

Regardless of what was actually agreed, what happened afterwards is well known. The commander, Giuseppe, along with twelve of his men, emerged from the fort with their flags rolled up and presented themselves to Grey. English troops were sent in to establish that the defenders had indeed laid down their arms and to secure and guard the munitions. Once the fort was secured, the 600 or so troops and the few accompanying women were taken to the place that has since earned the name of the Field of the Cutting (*Gort a' Ghearradh*) and executed one by one. The severed heads of the slain were apparently buried in the field where a monument stands today, while their bodies were thrown over the cliffs into the sea below.

After the massacre at Smerwick, the tide turned very much against the Desmonds and their rebellion. The coalition began to fall apart, although the war of attrition dragged on for another two years, with Desmond's supporters being killed or falling away with the offer of a pardon. In early 1582, John of Desmond was engaged by English troops and killed at the River Avonmore, his head sent to the now infamous Lord Grey.

Grey's brutality was notorious, but he had still not been successful in defeating the Geraldines. Possibly because of his cruel methods, Grey was recalled to England. The Fitzgerald's arch enemy the Earl of Ormonde replaced him as Lord Deputy, continuing on with the war that left much of Munster bereft of people, crops and livestock.

By the winter of 1583 the Earl of Desmond stood alone, with only a handful of supporters following him into the Slieve Mish mountains to elude English troops. It was here at Glenagenty that Gerald met his end. Desperate and hungry, he had stolen a few cattle from the Moriarty clan and supposedly mistreated the sister of the clan chief. Owen Moriarty and his men caught up with the earl at a small cabin, where he was killed and beheaded.

In return Moriarty received 1000 pounds of silver, a vast fortune, and Gerald's head was sent to Elizabeth in London, while his body was strung from the walls of Cork city for all to see. His title and all the Geraldine lands were confiscated by the English crown. Attempts to revive Desmond fortunes and the Earldom soon after were a failure and so the once powerful Geraldine dynasty came to a sad and miserable end.

NEXT PARISH: AMERICA

The breathtakingly beautiful archipelago of Na Blascaodaí, or the Blasket Islands as they have become better known, lie off the west coast of the Dingle Peninsula and form the most western extremity of Ireland. The six islands, namely An Blascaod Mór, Beiginis, Inis na Bró, Inis Mhic Uileáin, Inis Tuaisceart, and An Tiaracht, are so remote that it was said that the next parish over was America.

Up until the early 1950s, the islands supported a small but close-knit community of pure Gaels who toiled hard on land and sea and who kept the old ways alive. Indeed, the islands by their very location maintained a wonderful and unrivalled bastion of living heritage and ancient culture. At one point there was a thriving population of just over 175 people who were ruled over by their own king, but by the middle of the twentieth century, due to the unfortunate hardship of life and the reality of emigration, this had declined to just twenty-one ageing and elderly people and one young child.

The mighty Atlantic Ocean churned and chopped all around the little rocks, chiselling little flakes off from time to time – and although it supplied the islanders with their means of survival, it also regularly threatened their very existence. The ocean could cut off the island for days or weeks on end, and the poor residents had no option but to just sit tight and hope that their rations would not run out before Manannán Mac Lir calmed the waters once more.

Christmas was a joyous time on the islands and they made the best of what they had to celebrate such an important event in their calendar. It was in 1946 that they were all looking forward to the annual hurling match that took place on Christmas Day on the beach of Trá Bhán, where the women would watch from the dunes as the men competed by hitting the sliotar up and down the strand and in and out of the crystal clear waves.

After preparations were concluded and work was done in the fields on Christmas Eve, Seánín Ó Cearna, a strapping 24-year-old lad in the prime of his days, came home with his father. He suddenly didn't feel quite well and complained of a splitting head-ache, so sat down to rest for a moment on the settle-bed in the kitchen. The relief he obtained was short-lived, as he keeled over soon after onto the flagstone floor without warning or sound.

The family lay Seánín down in his father's bedroom and his sister Cáit went to fetch some water from Tobar na Croise, the nearby well, and also to heat a bag of flour to place on his forehead to ease the pain. She went to the nearby signalling station to make an urgent call for help with the island's battery-operated telephone, but this was not working and hadn't been for some time.

The gale-force winds and high waves were otherworldly, and so large that any attempt to cross the Sound to the mainland would be suicidal, so the only thing that the poor Ó Cearna family could do was to make Seánín comfortable and hope that his headache would ease and his flu would pass.

Unfortunately, his illness showed no sign of relief over the coming weeks and neither did the inclement weather outside. On 9 January he succumbed to his condition and slipped into an eternal sleep, much to the shock and distress of his family and the islanders.

As one storm ended and before another began, four local fishermen rowed over to the mainland in their neamhóg to acquire a coffin for his body and to send word of his death. The four men were able to get a coffin in Dingle, but had to transport it back by foot over rough and high ground to Dunquin, as the return crossing over the Sound was too rough for the little boat to endure. They met the lifeboat in Dunquin, who transferred them and the coffin over and waited to bring Seánín back for burial. He could not be buried on the Blaskets as the graveyard there was not consecrated.

The family accompanied Seánín's body back to the mainland, where an autopsy showed the cause of death not to be flu, but meningitis. When the doctor was filling out the death certificate his father said, with an equal measure of anger and grief in the little English he knew, 'Meningitis did not kill my boy, the Irish Government killed him!'

This heart-wrenching incident sent shivers down the backs of the islanders and they knew that life would only get harder for them. They wondered what hope they would have in an emergency if a healthy young man can be struck down suddenly and violently in his prime, and so they knew that they had to leave. They petitioned the government to be relocated to the mainland, but this continually fell on deaf ears until some six years later, when yet another prolonged storm forced the islanders to send an urgent telegram to the then Taoiseach, Eamon de Valera, seeking urgent help as they had all but run out of food.

Arrangements were made by the Irish Land Commission to transfer the remaining islanders to four newly built homes in Dunquin, on the opposite side of the Sound with a little land attached. They gathered at the little quay on the island with their furniture and other meager possessions, but the storms had reared up again and they had to leave their belongings behind. They left their otherworldly island home with a tear of sadness and a tear of happiness.

We shall never see the likes of the Blasket Islanders again.

The Gortaglanna Killings

A strange incident happened at Gortaglanna, in the valley of Knockanure, towards the end of the Irish War of Independence. The killings were the culmination of several skirmishes between the North Kerry IRA and Crown forces, and the incident was the inspiration of many poems and ballads, the most famous being *The Ballad of Gortaglanna.*

The ballads all tell basically the same sad story, but with some differences and distortions perhaps typical of romanticism being more exciting than the bald truth. Of the atrocity, only one of the four victims, by a combination of tenacity and good luck, managed to survive. His name was Cornelius 'Con' Dee, and it is mostly from him we know the truth of what happened, but this was only the sad end of a horrible set of incidents.

After the shooting of RIC officer O'Sullivan in January 1921, an IRA flying column of some twenty-five men was formed for North Kerry that successfully evaded attempts by the RIC, military and Black and Tans to capture them as they made their way across the county.

On 7 April, having received word of an army group returning to Listowel from the house of Sir Arthur Vicars in Kilmorna, the flying column decided to ambush them on the road. The ambush was not entirely successful, with Mick Galvin being shot dead by returning fire from the military, who were on bicycles. One soldier was killed and two wounded, and after an intense firefight the flying column was forced to withdraw, leaving Galvin behind.

A few days later, IRA Captain James Costello received orders for the flying column to execute Vicars and burn down his home. Vicars, who had been disgraced for negligently allowing the theft of the Irish Crown Jewels in Dublin, was believed to be a spy and military collaborator, and as such was sentenced to death by the IRA. The column stormed the house, setting fire to it with paraffin and petrol, and shot Vicars dead.

In retaliation, four shops were destroyed by the Black and Tans in Listowel on 27 April and the furious British authorities continued to desperately search for the IRA flying column. In later years, Con Dee would confirm that the flying column was temporarily disbanded at the beginning of May due to an outbreak of scabies among the men. It was decided that they break into groups of three or four in order to obtain medical treatment, before reforming again at a future date to be decided.

Con Dee, Paddy Walsh and Paddy Dalton made their way to Ballydonoghue, where Walsh said they could find a doctor. A dispatch from the IRA in Listowel reached the men, informing them that the police had got wind of a Redemptorist Mission in Athea that the West Limerick Column was planning to attend. It was decided that the three would travel to Athea with all due haste to ensure that the Limerick men would not fall into a police trap.

The unarmed men took a circuitous route on their way to Athea and met up with Josie Liston, who was able to forewarn them in time. Having come that far, the three men stayed three days in Athea to attend the devotions before setting out towards Listowel on the morning of 12 May.

Approaching the bridge at Gortaglanna, the three ran into Jerry Lyons on his bicycle, who stopped to exchange news. Fearing the possibility of police or worse, Paddy Walsh suggested that they leave the road and chat in an adjoining field where they would have more privacy. No sooner had they made it across the fence than they heard the sound of approaching lorries and Con Dee advised them all to take cover. Dee, Lyons and Dalton hit the ground as quickly as possible, while Paddy Walsh decided to run down to the end of the field before lying down. Most likely it was Walsh who was spotted by the convoy and before long, three of them were surrounded by the RIC, to be joined shortly by Walsh. Con Dee suggested that they come out with their hands up, which they did to a torrent of verbal abuse from their captors, who realised they'd probably caught members of the flying column.

After giving their names the four men were strip searched, but had nothing but a copy of the *Irish Independent* newspaper between them. While redressing themselves, the men were beaten with rifles and revolvers and savagely kicked as they lay on the ground. The four were separated some distance before each of them were set upon by four or five men. After twenty minutes of beatings, the men were huddled into three different lorries with Paddy Walsh and Paddy Dalton together in one of them.

After driving perhaps half a mile back towards Athea, the convoy stopped and turned around. Walsh and Dalton were put in with Dee before they set out again in the direction they had come from. This time they were driven for about a mile before being ordered to get out, all four of them battered and bloody. The men were asked to run, but knowing they might be shot for trying to escape they refused.

After another beating with rifles they were taken into a field by force and lined up facing the fence. Their protests for justice and demands that they face trial were laughed at by the Black and Tans, who called them murderers as they organised themselves into an impromptu firing squad. Con Dee watched as a Black and Tan rested his rifle on the fence directly in front of him while others did the same in front of his three comrades. A shot rang out and next to Dee, Jerry Lyons moaned, flinging up his arms as he fell backwards, hit in the chest.

As Con Dee saw the blood on Lyons' waistcoat he instinctively turned and ran into the field as fast as his legs could carry him. He didn't turn back to see the fate of his companions as the gunfire continued with bullets whizzing past. A bullet lodged in Con's right thigh but he ran on, albeit with a limp, for all he was worth. The RIC and Black and Tans gave chase, but Dee ran on for a mile and a half before pausing to discard his coat, collar, tie and puttees (over his boots). Pursued for another mile and a half, the exhausted Dee managed to elude the British forces by hiding in a drain in an oat garden.

Fortunately for Dee, after some forty-five minutes two local men came and helped him, but by now he wasn't able to walk more than 40 yards. One of the men was able to secure a car and take Con to a house about 2 miles outside Listowel. A young *Cumann na mBan* girl sought out Dr James Enright, who came to the house by pony and trap where he treated Con Dee for his leg injury.

Enright advised Dee to leave the area as soon as possible, as no doubt the authorities would be eager to catch the only witness of the executions. The three dead men – Paddy Walsh, Paddy Dalton and Jerry Lyons – were taken by the Black and Tans to Listowel and later identified in Tralee. Meanwhile, Cornelius Dee made good his escape and managed to remain in hiding until after the truce of July 1921.

Con moved to America and by strange coincidence met up with Dr Enright again in Chicago, about thirty years later, after Con's brother-in-law recognised him in a café. The following morning Con came to meet the doctor and presented him with a Scheaffer pen and stand in thanks for his help in 1921. In 1960, Con Dee came back to Ireland for a holiday, returning to Gortaglanna where he was photographed at the monument to his fallen comrades.

THE BRITISH ROYAL VISIT TO KERRY

In June 2018, the Prince of Wales and his wife Camilla visited Kerry, in what was the first British royal visit to the county in over 150 years. In doing so, Charles was retracing the steps of one of his most famous ancestors, Queen Victoria, who visited together with her family in 1861.

The queen had visited on two previous occasions, but the visit in '61 was to be her last. Accompanying her were her husband Prince Albert, and her children Alfred, Alice and Helena. After arriving in Dublin they visited their son Edward, who was attending army manoeuvres at the Curragh, before they took the royal train from Dublin's Kingsbridge station (now Heuston) direct to Killarney.

Unlike Victoria's earlier visits that had purpose (in 1849 to highlight the effects of the Great Famine and in 1853 to attend the Great Industrial Exhibition), this was primarily a private holiday for her family, though they still had their accompanying ladies-in-waiting and forty soldiers of the 1st Dragoons from the Curragh.

Disembarking at Killarney station in her mourning black (following the death of her mother in the spring), she was greeted by thousands of onlookers in the five purpose-built galleries and along the roads taken by the royal carriage. Despite her recent loss she appeared in good spirits and was greatly pleased by the warm reception she received from the public.

Victoria spent her first night in Killarney House, the then home of the Earl of Kenmare. This was very much a formal state occasion, with a lavish banquet attended by Kerry dignitaries and followed by an impressive firework display at the lower lake.

The following day, Victoria and her entourage made their way the few miles to Muckross House, home of the Herbert family. Embarking at Ross Castle, they travelled by an eight-oared barge around the upper and lower lakes for most of the day before arriving by carriage at Muckross Park in the evening.

The Muckross estate formerly belonged to the native MacCarthy Mór family, but had been in the hands of the Herberts since the 1700s. Lord Henry Arthur Herbert, who had formerly been Chief Secretary of Ireland and also built Muckross House, invested a huge sum in the restoration of the estate and a new road on the slopes of Mangerton in preparation for Victoria's visit.

No expense was spared and everything from servants' uniforms, china, linen and tapestries were commissioned especially for the occasion, although the royal party were to spend most of their time outside enjoying Kerry's magnificent scenery. On the following morning they toured the vast estate, taking in what became known as 'Ladies View'. This panoramic view, on the road to Kenmare, so impressed Victoria's ladies-in-waiting that the spot has since become one of the most famous and widely visited locations in the Killarney National Park.

The party also visited Dinis Island and Torc Waterfall before returning to their specially decorated apartments, which had been organised on the ground floor due to Victoria's fear of fire. After lunch they undertook another boat trip, in which the royal group went to Tomies to view a stag hunt that had been organised, although the hounds failed to catch anything.

On the final morning of the short two-night visit, Victoria visited the Franciscan ruins of Muckross Abbey, which had been closed by Oliver Cromwell in 1652. Very much impressed by its romantic appearance, its religious and political symbolism seemed to escape her.

Returning to Dublin by train after her whirlwind tour of Killarney, Victoria travelled through the crowd-lined capital city streets, noting 'many dirty ragged people running along near the carriage decidedly the worst for whisky'. This was probably her last vision of Ireland, perhaps the only glimpse of real life in what was otherwise a carefully orchestrated visit.

In November, those same streets were once more lined by the public, but this time for the funeral of Young Ireland activist Terence MacManus, a sure sign of the turning tide against British rule in Ireland. Shortly before Christmas that year, Victoria's beloved husband Albert died of typhoid, plunging her into deep mourning and a general withdrawal from public life.

Dublin Corporation's returning of a bust of Prince Albert, the refusal to accept a statue of Albert and refusal to rename St Stephen's Green to 'Albert Green' all led Victoria to feel deeply hurt and soured her views regarding Ireland and its people. By the end of the decade, with growing nationalist sentiments, the British monarchy's popularity in Ireland had declined dramatically and Victoria was never to return.

The Shannon Drownings of 1893

On 15 August 2018, a remembrance service took place at the Memorial Plaza in Tarbert, North Kerry, for the 125th anniversary of the tragedy that led to the loss of all seventeen souls aboard the Murphy's rowing boat that was ferrying passengers across the River Shannon. A plaque was erected there in 1988 and the tragedy has been marked every year since, but for the 125th anniversary a re-enactment took place in period costumes with a similar boat.

The names of those lost were Murphy (Maurice and his young son Paddy), Scanlon (sisters Mary, Katie, Bridget and brother Michael), Lyndon (Pat and sister Mary), Bovenizer (brothers Thomas and Michael), John Holly, Tom Glazier, Willie Naughton, Hannah O'Sullivan, Nora Fitzgerald, Ritchie Allen and Johanna McGrath, all of whom are listed on the memorial stone.

The Shannon Drownings tragedy, which was also known as the 'Drowning at Moyne', occurred in the evening as a group of boys and girls from Kerry returned by boat from Kilkee after a day trip. According to some, as many as twenty-one people were crammed into the rowing boat that left Tarbert. The fishing boat, owned by John Murphy, had been laid up previously at the end of the fishing season, and being constructed with butted planks instead of lapped may have dried out, causing it to take on water. With less than the usual number of boats available that day, the boat set out dangerously overloaded, especially considering it only had two oars.

After an enjoyable day, and against the advice of some of the locals, all except Catherine Holly took the Murphy boat back to Tarbert around 7.30 p.m. With the sunset due around 9 p.m., one-and-a-half hours should have been enough time to complete the return journey before it got dark. It is known that the boat was more than halfway across the Shannon when the accident happened, but nobody knows for certain the exact circumstances. However, it is said the inhabitants on the Clare side heard crying and shouting coming from the general location of Murphy's boat. Some think the boat may have missed its landing point, and people standing up to look for suitable landing spots may have caused it to capsize. Equally, a bad leak with nothing but shoes to bail out the water may have meant the boat succumbed to a sudden swell or was just too full of water. Indeed, many of the dead recovered were found with just one shoe, indicating that the boat was leaky.

With some very strong currents on the river there were no survivors. The bodies washed up on both the Kerry and Clare shores, but sadly five of the seventeen lost were never found. Bill Naughton's body was found at Carradotia. John Murphy's corpse was discovered near Querrin. Both Nora Fitzgerald and Patrick Linden were located near Kilrush Quay. Tom Gleasure's body washed up near Ryan's Point. Catherine Scanlan was found near Carrig Castle. The body of Tom Borbenizer was located near Tarbert lighthouse and his brother Michael's corpse was found on the Tarbert shore. The five dead whose bodies were never found were Mary Linden, Johanna McGrath, Patrick Murphy, Bridget and Michael Scanlan. Tarbert town went into deep mourning for a period of six days while the burials were taking place one by one.

The tragedy is remembered in both song and poetry and a local account recorded in the following century.

2

LEGENDARY FIGURES AND FAMOUS PEOPLE

BRENDAN AND THE ELUSIVE ISLE OF THE BLESSED

One of the greatest frontier men and pioneers of overseas travel to have come out of Kerry was our very own St Brendan. He was a gentle and sacred man, with a strong affinity and respect for water and for travelling over its waves to other lands to spread the word of God.

He is known far and wide as someone who was an experienced seafarer and adventurer, and stories of his many journeys and magical encounters have fascinated young and old for well over 1,000 years. In his little coracle he sailed over to Wales, Scotland, Brittany and around many parts of Ireland, establishing religious communities and shrines along the way – his greatest being at Ardfert in Kerry and Clonfert in Galway.

Brendan was born in the area known as the Marsh of Ambrose, near the southern edge of Tralee Bay. It was in the early fifth century that he first graced the world with his holy presence; it is said that brightly lit angels hovered over his parents' home during the labour. Baptised by St Erc in the famed well at Tubrid, near Ardfert, he went on at the age of 26 to take holy orders and was ordained a priest, also by Erc.

Many people think that Brendan landed in America many, many years before Christopher Columbus. The story of this, his greatest adventure, began in the mid fifth century, when his friend St Barrid told him of a very special place that he himself had visited. This place was known by many names, chief among them being Hy Brasail – Isle of the Blessed, the Garden of Eden, or in more recent years, St Brendan's Island. Barrid explained: 'in this magical place day never ends, every rock is a diamond, every tree laden down with edible fruits, every plant full of flowers, and the weather is always warm and pleasant. It truly is a jewel.'

To an adventurer such as Brendan, he had heard all he needed to and went about making immediate arrangements to find this place. On the coast near the base of Mount Brandon, he and fourteen monks built a traditional currach of wattle and hides, tanned with oak bark and softened with butter. They set a single mast and sail, and, after some time fasting and praying, fearlessly set off out into the bay in the direction of the wild Atlantic Ocean.

Just as they passed Fenit, three men called out to the monks and begged to be taken with them on their voyage. Brendan scoffed and said, 'Ach, sure why would we be bringing three non-believers, when we have the perfect number here already?' But his friends persuaded him otherwise, and so he reluctantly agreed to let them come.

They were sailing for many weeks and they became very hungry, as they had not seen land in some time and their limited rations were already running low. Suddenly they saw a low-lying sandy spit rise up in the middle of the salt water ahead of them. In the centre of this small island was an equally small house, circular in shape. In the hope of food, they pulled their currach up onto the beach and were surprised to be met by a dog, wagging his tail. The men were all amazed when the dog opened his mouth but instead of barking, he cheerily greeted them and said '*Fáilte, a chairde*! Welcome, friends!'

They were all dumbstruck, but came on shore and followed the dog as they were bid. The dog explained that they had landed on Mysterious Island and that they could eat and drink as much as they desired, but they must not touch anything else on the land.

They went into the house, which was bigger on the inside than it looked on the outside. It was filled with the most marvellous furnishings, with fine paintings hanging from the walls and the most expensive rugs on the floor. In the main room was a large circular table in the middle, set out with an abundance of bread, fruit and beer, with just as many chairs around the table as there were people present. They thought this strange, but the hunger took over and they dropped what they had in their hands and began gorging on the lovely food.

One of the non-believers, when he had had his fill, sneaked out of the back door and took a walk along the barren island. He noticed that there were no humans on the island and nothing was growing there either, apart from a solitary mangled hawthorn at the far end. He walked over and saw a gold chain hanging from one of the branches. 'I'll have that for myself!' he thought, and stuffed the chain into his tunic pocket. Just as he did this, the tree shook and a large demon arose from the trunk.

'After the hospitality I have generously provided, you re-pay me with theft?' The non-believer was terrified and opened his mouth to apologise to the demon but no words would come out.

By this time, Brendan and the rest of the men had come out of the house and could see what was happening. The demon turned into a fine mist and suddenly entered through the non-believer's mouth, possessing his body. His eyes rolled backwards in his head and he fell to the ground screaming in unearthly tones. Brendan ran over to the spot and prayed over the man's body in an effort to exorcise the demon, but before exiting the body once more, the demon laughed and said, 'I have made it so you will not return to Ireland for seven full years!' and with that he suddenly left with a terrifying shriek, flying back into the tree. The non-believer was at this point dead. They had a funeral for the man and buried him on the island before pushing the currach back out into the surf and setting sail once more for the west.

The monks and the two remaining non-believers continued on their journey through turbulent seas and driving winds, when all of a sudden the rain stopped, the sea calmed and a thick fog rose up all around them. In the near distance, they could make out the outline of a hunched figure, sitting on a rock in the middle of the ocean. As they got closer, they were horrified to see that one side of this man's body was frozen solid and the other side was in flames. They had not seen anything of the likes in all their lives.

The man, writhing in agony, said, 'I am Judas Iscariot. I have been sentenced to an eternity in hell for my betrayal of Jesus of Nazareth. My only respite is to sit on this rock on Sundays and Feast Days.' Brendan felt sorry for Judas and so prayed to God to protect him for one night from the torments of hell, which God granted. They stayed with Judas until the morning and then continued on their way.

The temperature then suddenly dropped and they all felt the cold in their bones. Passing a rocky island covered in snow-covered mountains, they could see demons running around hurling fiery slag onto the land and into the surrounding waters. Rivers of hot gold flowed from the mountain tops. Surrounding the island were countless huge white pillars of crystal floating all around them in the waters.

Brendan pointed to the largest spewing mountain top and declared that this was '*An Uaimh go hIfreann*! The Cave to Hell!'

Suddenly Brendan and his currach got the demons' unwelcome attentions and they began scooping up lava and throwing balls of fire at them. The holy boat evaded each missile. Just then, a demon took a standing jump from the island over to the boat and landed on the shoulders of the second non-believer, sinking its sharp claws into his flesh. They fought and struggled, but eventually the demon dragged him off the currach, across the water and onto the island. The combination of heat and cold caused untold pain to the poor man and he was taken up to the mountain top and then straight down to hell.

After this exhausting and upsetting ordeal, the men felt overwhelmed. They found a black shiny mass in the ocean and decided to tie up here and rest for the night. They lay down and were soon asleep on the warm spongy ground. The following morning, they arose and gathered some driftwood to make a small fire to cook some fish for their breakfast. They lit the sticks and fanned the flames until they had a fine roaring fire going, onto which they placed the fish to cook.

Suddenly, the ground began to tremble and shudder, and out of nowhere a huge geyser shot from the earth high into the sky. The monks equally began to tremble, but in fear. They left their fire and food and ran for the boat. The island began to sink into the ocean, and on looking back from behind saw that it was not an island they had camped on at all, but a huge whale!

Elena Danaan

They next found an island populated by three anchorite monks, who provided nourishment for the weary travellers. The third non-believer was so impressed with their compassion and faith that he decided to convert and remain with them.

The voyage continued for some time longer, but they eventually landed at their desired location of the Isle of the Blessed. It was so large that they could not explore it in 100 lifetimes; it was everything they had hoped for and more. It truly was paradise on Earth. It is believed by many to this day that the Isle of the Blessed was in fact North America and that Brendan was the first European to set foot on it, and not Christopher Columbus.

Much archaeological evidence of apparent Irish influence has been found in North America and continues to be found, and there are also stories of a white Irish-speaking tribe. Who can say for sure?

After a life of adventure, St Brendan died in 578 at Annaghdown while visiting his sister. He had become such a superstar of Early Christian Ireland that he was worried his body would be stolen by relic hunters, so he arranged for his body to be secretly placed into a luggage cart and transported back to his beloved Clonfert, where he is still buried to this day.

MARIE ANTOINETTE AND RICE HOUSE

Marie Antoinette is possibly one of the most well-known queens in world history, but her connection with the town of Dingle is a piece of Irish history that is hardly known outside of Kerry. A plaque erected on the wall of Rice House in 2010 by Dingle Historical Society was unveiled by the Austrian Ambassador to Ireland. Apart from this small commemoration, there is little to acknowledge the rescue attempt that could have saved the French queen's life, which was just one of several such failed plans to rescue her.

The plan to save her was organised by James Louis Rice, the son of 'Black' Tom Rice, who was a successful wine merchant from Ballymacdoyle, close to Dingle town. Tom had built up extensive connections with traders and vineyards throughout both Spain and France. James, born in 1730 into a Catholic family, was educated at the Irish Pastoral College in Louvain, Belgium as there were few educational opportunities in Ireland due to penal laws against Catholics. James did well in Belgium and even began studying for the priesthood at the Franciscan seminary in Louvain. However, he abandoned his studies and went on to join the Irish brigade of the Austrian (Hapsburg) army, becoming a cavalry officer, and was later made a Count of the Holy Roman Empire by the Austrian Emperor Joseph II, who he had met and befriended at military academy.

Rice even gained a seat on the Emperor's privy council and was one of the trusted soldiers honoured with escorting Joseph's younger sister, Marie Antoinette, from Vienna to Versailles in May 1770 to join her new husband, Louis XVI of France. James remained in Paris, in service of the royal family, but retained his contacts with his friend Emperor Joseph into the 1780s, while the situation in France deteriorated in the run-up to the revolution in 1789.

After the death of Joseph II, his younger brother Leopold became Emperor of Austria and it was his support, and that of his sister for the French monarchy, that led to France declaring war on Austria in 1792. Louis XVI was separated from Marie Antoinette and their two remaining children, who were themselves imprisoned in the tower of the temple in Marais. At the behest of Leopold, James Rice began planning an audacious attempt to rescue Marie Antoinette – or Maria Antonia as her brother would have called her.

The plan was to bribe the guards at the temple and take her and any other members of the royal family by carriage and a relay of horses to Nantes. From there, a merchant ship, owned by the Rice family business, would take them to Dingle. The Rice family went so far as to furnish rooms in their Dingle home in readiness for the Bourbon monarchy, although the plan was to eventually send them to London and then on to safety in Vienna, with her brother Leopold, the Austrian Emperor.

Rice enlisted the help of Thomas Trant, a man from Ventry serving with the Irish Brigade in France, William Hickie, from Ballylongford, and Count Waters of Paris, who was married to his sister, Mary Rice. Although the plan went off well initially, Marie Antoinette, who was held separately from her husband and two children, refused to leave her family and so the escape had to be abandoned.

After the abolition of the monarchy, Louis XVI was tried, found guilty of treason and executed at the guillotine in January 1793. After Marie's transfer to the Conciergerie, a final rescue attempt, which became known as the Carnation Plot, was attempted, but unfortunately also failed. The former Queen, in failing health, was executed in October of that same year.

James Rice was able to escape from France and moved to London, after which he served in the allied forces, which consisted primarily of Britain, Austria, Russia and Spain, in the first of the French Revolutionary Wars. This conflict was known as the War of the First Coalition, which ended in 1797 with the humiliation of Austria by the French.

In the late 1790s, Rice returned to his native Ireland and settled in Limerick, during which he witnessed the United Irishmen's rising of 1798 and the emergence of Daniel O'Connell as a political force. He died at the age of 61 in 1801, as Napoleon continued his rise to power and eventual victory in the War of the Second Coalition.

Count James Louis Rice's death was widely reported, both in Ireland and across Europe, having become quite a hero among monarchists during those turbulent times.

Rice House, which was built in the 1750s, came into the possession of the Catholic Church and was used as a presbytery, but it eventually came into the ownership of *Údarás na Gaeltachta*. A subsequent plan to redevelop and sell the house came up against considerable opposition, due to what would have been the effective gutting of the interior with additions and modernisations of the exterior. Most of the original features of the house, including the rooms prepared for Marie Antoinette, were still in excellent condition, leading to a campaign to keep the historical building in its near-pristine state.

Largely due to the work of the Rice House Alliance, planning permission was revoked and the house became a listed building in 2004. It was then sold to a local businessman from Dingle, and today Rice House is home to Kerry Education and Training Board and, albeit partially modernised, thankfully still retains its unique features and period character.

Brian Boru and the Battle of Affouley

The most revered High King ever to have ruled the land was a native of the Dál gCais by the name of Brian Borumha, better known to many today as Brian Boru. He was born in the mid tenth century, in the area now occupied by the village of Killaloe in County Clare.

In the early years of his life Brian was sent off to receive his education at a religious house, as was common with children of royal lineage, and he completed this on the famed island of Inis Faithlinn in Loch Léin, Killarney. It was while he was there that he received word of a Danish Viking raid on his village, far away on the banks of the Shannon. He heard that the Danes had come from Limerick and sacked the settlement, burning all of its buildings to the ground and carrying off the women for their own ends. Brian's own father was hit in the back with a Danish axe and died of his wounds, with neither a physician nor priest by his side.

Following the untimely death of Brian's father, the kingship of Thomond had passed to his brother, who was not long on the throne when he, too, was murdered by the Vikings in a further raid.

Life was by no means easy in those days; it came and went all too quickly. In no time at all, Brian found himself holding the kingship of Thomond and subsequently the crown of all-Munster. These things were not earned without great bloodshed, and by this stage in his life Brian had learned much in the ways of combat and leadership – and had developed a deep hatred of the Danes for what they had done to his brethren.

One autumn day, a few of the Dál gCais men were out chopping down some trees to repair and replace a number of the rotten posts on the perimeter of the small military fort at Affouley, not far from Lisselton. They were busy skinning the bark from the freshly felled trunks when they heard a number of men walking nearby. They were laughing and talking in a language that the Dál gCais men did not know.

The men of the Dál gCais knew that there was something amiss and so to be on the safe side they sent for King Brian, who was resting nearby. When he heard, the king arose and came as quickly as he could. Listening to the brogue of the men he knew instantly that they were Danes and were up to no good, as such men do not simply go on holidays to Ireland.

Brian bade the men be silent and they all sneaked up behind the Danes. He pulled his long sword from its scabbard and quietly placed it through the bushes that grew between the two enemies. Quickly and swiftly, he spun himself around to face the opposite direction, severing the branches of the trees and also the heads of several of the men in the process.

The remaining Danes arose in shock at what had happened and, brandishing their axes, they started to battle with the men. Arms and legs were cut off and the battle was hard-fought and bloody. The spirit of the Danes was finally broken at dusk by the superior might of the Gaels, and the invaders fled in fear for their lives.

Ensuring honour in death as in life, the men buried the fallen Danes inside the fort at Affouley, and this place can be seen to this day.

The Last Knight of Kerry

The Knight of Kerry (alternatively 'The Green Knight') is one of three ancient Hiberno – Norse hereditary knighthoods created by the first Baron Desmond, John Fitzgerald. The other two titles were the White Knight and Knight of Glin (alternatively 'The Black Knight'), although both of these are now extinct.

After the death of his first wife, John re-married to Honora, daughter of Hugh O'Connor of Kerry. He had three sons with Honora, who could not inherit his Barony, which would go to his first son. As a Count Palatine he had the right to create knighthoods for his three younger sons, which were passed on down the generations.

The White Knights established in Limerick and Kilkenny began with Maurice Fitzgibbon, grandson of Baron Desmond, although this knighthood ended in 1611 with the death of the 12th White Knight (another Maurice) who had no children. Attempts have since been made, unsuccessfully, to claim the title.

The Knights of Glin bore the name Fitzgerald, the first being Sir John Fitz-John Fitzgerald, who built the family's castle on the Shannon estuary in County Limerick. Despite a certain rebelliousness, including towards Elizabeth I, the knights continued after the destruction of the castle into the twenty-first century. The final knight, Desmond Fitzgerald, still lived at the Glin manor close to the original castle, but died there of cancer in 2011, leaving three daughters and no sons to inherit the title.

The last surviving Irish knight is Adrian Fitzgerald, the last Knight of Kerry. The Knights of Kerry once owned Rathinane Castle, built inside an ancient rath overlooking both Ventry and Dingle bays, the ruins of which can still be seen today. From the late eighteenth century, the Knights of Kerry also resided at Valentia Island. Adrian's ancestor, Sir Peter Fitzgerald, 19th Knight of Kerry, was instrumental in the creation of the seaport, railway terminal, the building of Knightstown and the transatlantic cable – used for the first telegraph message sent from America to Europe.

Adrian Fitzgerald, now in his late seventies, is a distant cousin of the last Knight of Glin, Desmond Fitzgerald, who he knew well and considered a friend. Interviewed after Desmond's death, Adrian expressed his sadness at not just being the last of three Irish Knights but also the last Knight of Kerry, a title that has been handed down for over 700 years.

Like his distant cousin Desmond, Adrian, who is also Baronet of Valencia, has no sons and as 24th Knight of Kerry, will be the last. He was born in Britain in 1940, where his father George was serving as an officer in the army during the Second World War. He became a Conservative Party politician and was Mayor of Kensington in the 1980s. He is retired now and divides his time between London and his estate in County Waterford.

MURDER OF THE COLLEEN BAWN

A shebeen or sibín was a place where alcohol was made and sold without a licence. Usually poitín was the drink of choice in these places, as it was cheap to make and the raw materials were plentiful. These shebeens were located in remote and lonely places as they were illegal establishments, and the police were always on the lookout for hidden stills and curious gatherings.

Some say that there was a shebeen in Rusheen and some say it was in Carraig, but whichever was the case one thing is certain: a truly dreadful chain of events started from it.

Ellen Hanley was a spritely young lass of 15 years of age. She was known far and wide for her blinding beauty and her convivial personality. This attracted the attentions of many a suitor, but one in particular, a John Scanlon, was particularly taken with the young Ellen, as she was with him. In no time at all the couple were courting and things went from strength to strength.

In Ellen's eyes life could not get any better, but when John proposed marriage to her after just a short time together she thought she was in heaven. In the summer of 1819 they eloped together and spent six long weeks together as husband and wife – but it was to end all too horribly.

John was a member of the upper classes, and although it did not matter to him in the beginning, Ellen's lower 'status' in society began to grate on him. He soon grew tired of her, and as divorce was not an option, the only other way out was on the

death of one of them. He decided it was going to be Ellen. He hatched a plan with one Stephen Sullivan, a man employed as his servant, and they agreed that Sullivan would take Ellen out in John's boat for a wee trip on the River Shannon.

Ellen thought the idea of a boat trip to be a splendid one, but little did she know that Sullivan had brought a gun and hidden it in his jacket to be used to murder her. They set out on to the Shannon for their little trip and Sullivan tried and tried to muster the nerve to go through with the shooting, but he was just not able to compose himself enough to do it and so turned the boat around to return to shore with Ellen. John saw the boat approaching from a distance and was expecting to see Sullivan row in alone as it got nearer, but became furious when he saw the two returning. He told Ellen to go for a walk while he brought Sullivan to the local shebeen.

At the shebeen, John plied Sullivan full of the illicit substance to make it easier for him to go through with the deed, and not before Sullivan was ossified did John call Ellen back and sweet talk her into taking another boat trip. She began to suspect something was up but reluctantly agreed, and so she departed in the boat once more with a quite inebriated Sullivan. This time around he had no problem in finishing the ghastly deed, and he tied a large rock to the poor girl's body and threw it into the waters, watching as it sank into the murky depths.

Just a few weeks later, the body of the poor innocent girl washed up at Moneypoint near Kilrush in County Clare, and the realisation of what had happened caused shivers and outrage through all levels of society.

Although the two men went on the run, they were both captured shortly afterwards. John Scanlan hired the great Daniel O'Connell to represent him in court and thought that his high status would save him from the hangman's noose. He was sorely mistaken, and swung from the end of the rope on Gallow's Green, Clare, in March 1820, while Sullivan was also put to death in Limerick.

Ellen Hanley became known worldwide as the Colleen Bawn (*Cailín Bán*), which translates from the Irish as 'Fair Girl'. She is buried in Burrane Cemetery not far from Kilrush, and her grave is inscribed with the following epitaph:

Here lies the Colleen Bawn,
Murdered on the Shannon,
July 14th 1819. R.I.P.

Oisín and the Land of Tír na n-Óg

Oisín was known far and wide as the greatest poet in all of Ireland. He was also talented in matters of love and war, holding a special place in the hearts of many women and also in the ranks of the mighty Fianna, personal army of the High King.

The hero of our story was conceived following the hunt of his mother Sadhbh by his father, the mighty Fionn MacCumhaill.

Now, his father was not usually in the habit of hunting down women, but Sadhbh was not in the form of a woman. She had been transformed into a deer by the evil druid, Fear Doirche, which accurately translates as 'Dark Man'. When Fionn caught up with Sadhbh, he looked into her eyes and saw in them something that told him that she was no animal. At that moment, the spell was broken, Sadhbh transformed back into her human form and they both fell in love.

Oisín was the fruit of this union and his life was anything but boring. One day, while resting during a hunt with his comrades at the royal forests of Killarney, he began to recite one of his otherworldly poetic compositions. His skill was subtle but powerful, and all who listened could not help but be captivated and enthralled. His recital was interrupted by the 'clip clop' from the hooves of a horse approaching from the distance. As this was restricted land, the Fianna jumped up in readiness of a conflict but were surprised to see something they did not expect. On a shining white mare rode the most beautiful woman any of them had ever seen; her hair was golden and her skin the palest of white. She wore a dress the colour of the night sky, studded with stars that could have come from the heavens themselves. A wonderful aura surrounded her and her whole being radiated goodness. Realising she was no threat, the Fianna lowered their weapons as she approached, and she spoke to them in a soft voice.

'I am Niamh of the Golden Hair, fairy woman and daughter of Manannán Mac Lir, God of the Sea. I have come to speak with Oisín, great poet of the Fianna.'

The poet stood up and they walked along the edge of Loch Léin and talked. Niamh had told him that she had heard of his skill as a true Irish *file* or poet and that she would like to hear more.

He said to Niamh, 'I am bound by duty to my comrades and the Fianna on this day, but I will meet you here at the Lake of Learning during the next full moon and I shall recite for you then.'

Elena Danaan

Loch Léin, or Lake of Learning, is the largest of the three Lakes of Killarney. It is located in an area of outstanding beauty and ancient history, with its name deriving from the centre of learning that once existed for many years on the island of Inis Faithlinn. Legend dictates that this island is the location where Brian Boru, High King of Ireland, received his education.

It was just over a week later from Oisín's initial meeting with Niamh, when the moon was full and the night sky was lit up by its glow. The broad loch of Munster shimmered in the moonlight and the poet rested on the banks while he awaited the arrival of his fairy lady. He heard the now familiar sound of Niamh's horse Embarr's hooves – but they were not cantering over the land, they were coming in over the surface of the mighty loch as if it were as solid as the earth.

'Recite for me,' she asked of Oisín, and he began to recite a most beautiful poem he had composed about Niamh. Before he had finished, they had both fallen deeply in love with each other and spent the night together on the edge of the lake.

The following morning, Niamh declared to Oisín, 'It would make me immensely happy if you would come home with me to Tír na n-Óg. My land is a place of everlasting youth and promise, a magical place covered in perpetual blooms where nobody grows old or ever gets ill, everybody is happy and healthy, and nobody has any wants.' She went on to explain, 'I cannot live without you, but as I am a fairy woman, I cannot stay in the human world, but, as a human man, you may live with me in the otherworld. My father is also the King of Tír na n-Óg.'

Oisín did not know how to respond to this as it was quite a predicament to be put in! He knew that he also could not live without Niamh, but he would have to leave his father and all of his friends in the Fianna, so he asked her to give him one night to think about it and to ask Fionn for advice.

He returned to speak with his father back at his fort on the Hill of Almu and discussed the situation with him.

Fionn was not best pleased but, being a wise man himself who had lived a full life, he understood the complexities of love, and so gave his blessing on the condition that Oisín return in the not too distant future, which he duly agreed and promised.

The following day, the lovers met once more at the loch and, climbing up on Niamh's horse, they galloped away over the land. Taking one great and final leap at Glenbeigh, they were out into the waves to Tír na n-Óg.

Tír na n-Óg was everything that Oisín could ever have imagined and so much more. Both he and Niamh were immensely happy and their love grew from strength to strength. Niamh bore two children by Oisín: a boy, Oscar, and a girl, Plúr na mBan, meaning Flower of Women. He lived among the sídhe, spending his days as they did in hunting, feasting, drinking, and love making.

After just three years of bliss, a longing developed within Oisín to visit his beloved Ireland and friends in the Fianna, but most of all to see his father once more. He spoke with Niamh and, knowing the implications of such a visit, she pleaded with him to stay with her. He reluctantly agreed but this was short-lived as the sadness in him grew, something unheard of in Tír na n-Óg. Niamh knew that she would have to relent and allow Oisín to return to Ireland for a visit, but she also knew that all would not be as he left it. Niamh warned him that he may travel on Embarr over the waves to Ireland, but he must not under any circumstances dismount or allow his feet to touch the earth, as it would mean that he would never be able to return to her. In his excitement he agreed, but he didn't really listen. He immediately began to make preparations for his trip.

Embarr was prepped, saddled and ready for departure. Oisín kissed his children, Oscar and Plúr na mBan, and his beloved Niamh and promised to return in the not too distant future. They all waved him goodbye, and the tear in Niamh's eye was from the realisation that what awaited Oisín in Ireland would not be what he expected and would certainly not ease his longing for the people and place that he left behind.

Oisín and Embarr reached Ireland at Glenbeigh, from where he and Niamh had departed just three years earlier – or so he thought. As they galloped along to Loch Léin he looked around and became angry to see that large swathes of the mighty oak forests of Killarney had been felled.

'Who dared to fell the hunting grounds of the Fianna?' he thought. 'Whoever is responsible will be punished!' Where the forests once grew, large parts were nothing more than open fields where animals grazed or where vegetables grew. He wondered how all of this damage could have been done in the three short years since he left. He galloped onwards to the fort of Fionn and the training grounds of the Fianna at Almu. Along the way he saw that the people of Ireland had become small, withered and weak, and when he arrived at Almu, he found that the entire place was deserted. The plain where he had trained since childhood was overgrown with types of trees that he had never seen before and the whole area was flooded. The fort on the Hill of Almu was in ruins, with ivy growing through the stones and windows. He found men quarrying sand and stone from the side of the hill. Oisín could not deal with any of this and the sorrow in him grew worse than if he had never visited. He thought that one person would surely know what was happening and that would be the High King himself at Tara.

He set off for the Hill of Tara to get answers. As he passed through Gleann na Smól or Valley of the Thrushes, where he had also hunted on many an occasion in the past, he saw two men building a road and having some difficulty in moving a large rock. Oisín stopped and began bragging, in typical Fianna fashion, that he could move this rock with just one hand. The men would not believe him, and so he reached down from the horse and lifted the rock with one hand, as he had bragged. Just as he had the rock up at chest height, the saddle girth snapped and he lost his balance, falling to the ground. In an instant, he grew to be a very, very old man.

Elena Danaan

The men brought the now very old Oisín to a holy man known as Patrick, who spoke with him. Oisín asked, 'Where is Fionn MacCumhaill, my father, and the Fianna?' Patrick explained that the Fionn and the Fianna had not existed in 300 years. Everything then made sense, and Oisín realised at this point that he had not been away for three years, but for 300 years. He was sad to see what had happened to Ireland and also that he would never see his father, his friends, or his family again. He died at this point and was taken to the Glens of Antrim, where he was laid to rest and a large cairn erected over his grave, which can be seen to this day.

THE O'RAHILLY

Michael Joseph Rahilly was born in 1875, the son of a wealthy Catholic grocer and landowner in Ballylongford, who went on to become one of the great heroes of the Easter Rising in 1916.

Rahilly was educated in Ballylongford before studying in a Jesuit boarding school in Kildare until 1893, when he returned to Kerry briefly and met American Nancy Brown, who he would later marry. She was studying in Paris and was only on holiday in Kerry. While studying at Royal University of Ireland (now UCD), Michael used his winnings from betting on a horse race to visit her in Paris. After her studies, Nancy returned to America and they remained in contact only by letter until 1898.

After his father's death in 1896, Michael abandoned his studies to take over the family business. Like his father before him, Michael served as a Justice of the Peace although not for very long – on hearing that Nancy had been proposed to he decided to sell the family business and the two houses in Ballylongford. Michael went first to Amsterdam, where he bought an engagement ring, before taking a ship to New York in September of 1898. Fortunately for him, Nancy accepted his proposal. They were married in April the following year and the couple honeymooned by taking a grand tour of Europe.

They continued to live in New York, where Rahilly expressed his growing nationalism in a letter to the *New York Herald*, criticizing the 80th birthday celebrations for Queen Victoria.

It was in New York that his first child, Bobby, was born in 1900. The family then returned to Ireland in 1902, where Michael resumed his position as a Justice of the Peace and a second child, Mac, was born in 1903. Around this time,

Michael became interested in researching his family ancestry, which would prove significant in years to come. He moved briefly to London in 1904, where he was involved in the United Irish League and the Irish Home Rule Party and where a third son, Aodogán, was born. Their time in London was brief, with the family moving back to America again in 1905, this time to Philadelphia, to help with the family woollen mill business.

While in America Michael kept his eye on the political situation in Ireland, and when his friend James O'Mara left the Irish Home Rule Party to join Sinn Féin, Rahilly did likewise. On their return to Ireland in 1909, the family settled in Dublin, with Michael increasingly referring to himself as Mícheál Ua Rathaille or O'Rahilly as he became more involved in Sinn Féin and traced his ancestral connections to the eighteenth-century Gaelic poet Aodhagán Ó Rathaille.

Adopting the styling of ancient Celtic chieftains, as the oldest living male in the family Michael began to refer to himself as 'The O'Rahilly' or 'Ua Rathaille', the name that he is generally remembered by, although he was not from a noble or royal line.

With an independent income of £900 a year, The O'Rahilly was able to make donations to Sinn Féin and also support and write for Arthur Griffith's Sinn Féin newspaper. He became increasingly vocal and both wrote and spoke in public against the coronation and royal visit of George V to Ireland in 1911. He also became Assistant Editor of the nationalist Gaelic League newspaper.

After the Ulster Volunteer Force was formed, The O'Rahilly and Eoin MacNeill created the Irish Volunteers in 1913 to defend Home Rule and to secure and maintain the rights and liberties of Ireland. It grew rapidly to some 200,000 members, but against the wishes of its founders it became controlled by John Redmond and the Irish Parliamentary Party. When the British banned the importing of weapons into Ireland The O'Rahilly, together with Roger Casement, Erskine Childers and Bulmer Hobson, organised 1,500 Mauser rifles to be delivered to Howth for the Irish Volunteers in July 1914.

The First World War caused a major split within the ranks of the Irish Volunteers over concerns about the establishment of the Home Rule Act, leading to the majority of members leaving with John Redmond to form the National Volunteers, who supported fighting for Britain against Germany.

A much-reduced Irish Volunteers carried on with The O'Rahilly as Director of Arms and with closer links to the Irish Republican Brotherhood, which began preparing for a future insurrection against British rule. The O'Rahilly and MacNeill were against instigating armed action unless it had some realistic chance of success, unlike their IRB comrades, who were determined to organise an uprising while the First World War continued.

Padraig Pearse ordered three days of manoeuvres over Easter 1916, which was really a cover for the IRB-planned uprising. With the failure of the German arms shipment to Kerry on Good Friday, MacNeill countermanded Pearse's orders in the belief that the Rising would be a disaster. The O'Rahilly, in support of MacNeill, drove around much of the country issuing orders for the Volunteers not to mobilise before returning, exhausted, to Dublin on Sunday.

However, his efforts only succeeded outside Dublin, for when he returned he found his colleagues were determined and that the Rising was only delayed by a day. Resigned to the situation, he is famously quoted to have said: 'Well, I've helped to wind up the clock, I might as well hear it strike!' and 'It is madness but it is glorious madness', joining his comrades at the GPO where the Irish Republic proclamation was read out by Pearse.

The O'Rahilly took command on the top floor of the GPO, which was pounded remorselessly by artillery and machine-gun fire, until eventually he led an attempt to break through British forces. He led his men out towards Moore Street, intending to regroup at a factory on Great Britain (now Parnell) Street, but they quickly ran into trouble due to a barricade and machine-gun post on Moore Street.

Accounts vary, but it's certain that The O'Rahilly led the ill-fated charge up Moore Street before being shot down. According to Tom Devine, he was ahead of the men and was shot and killed there on Moore Street. According to others (and his own note), he managed to shelter in a doorway, having taken bullets to the shoulder and hip, before managing to make it to the corner of Sackville Street where he collapsed. One account from ambulance man Albert Mitchel claims that the British Army would not allow him medical assistance, but others have suggested that with the confusion and constant machine-gun fire, it was impossible for him to gain assistance from either side. Whatever the case, The O'Rahilly lived long enough to write a note on the back of a letter from his son Aodhagán, which already had a bullet hole through it.

> Written after I was shot - Darling Nancy, I was shot leading a rush up Moore Street took refuge in a doorway. While I was there I heard the men pointing out where I was & I made a bolt for the lane I am in now. I got more [than] one bullet I think. Tons and tons of love dearie to you & to the boys & to Nell & Anna. It was a good fight anyhow. Please deliver this to Nannie O'Rahilly, 40 Herbert Park, Dublin. Good bye Darling.

A British officer found the note, which was delivered to his beloved wife Nancy, who was pregnant with their fourth child. The O'Rahilly is remembered as one of the bravest commanders of the Rising and was buried in Glasnevin Cemetery, in what was to become a plot for heroes of the Republic. Sackville Lane was renamed O'Rahilly Parade in his honour and The O'Rahilly is forever immortalised in William Butler Yeats' poem 'Sing Of The O'Rahilly', written in 1938.

DAN THE FEATHERS: THE ROBIN HOOD OF MUNSTER

The last true heir to the kingship of Desmond was a colourful character by the name of Dónal MacCarthy. He lived in sixteenth-century Killarney and such was the impact he had on that place, that he is said to still visit on a nightly basis to this very day.

Known to his friends as Dan, he spent his time attacking the English whenever he came across them. He particularly enjoyed burning the planters off 'their' land and returning the land back to the Irish it was originally taken from. One habit of his was to collect the feathers from the plume helmets worn by the Queen's Guards he had attacked. It is said that he slept on a mattress filled with these feathers, which earned him the nickname among the Irish of 'Dan the Feathers.'

Even when word spread among the common man and woman of England of his charitable and brave efforts in restoring the rights of his own country people, he was not so much hated as he was respected, and they honoured him with the nickname of 'Robin Hood of Munster.' By contrast, the stiff English upper classes who made the rules knew that Dan was a threat to their ambitions and put a bounty on his head. He was a hard man to find at the best of times, but they soon realised that he was nigh on impossible to capture due to his excellent knowledge of his native land and his ability to vanish without a trace after his many raids.

Like Robin Hood of Nottingham, some began to wonder if Dan was a ghostly apparition, or if he was just a myth and never even existed at all!

The English had outlawed the Brehon Law system not long before, and replaced this organic system with their own foreign laws. Under the English system, Dan could not be inaugurated as King of Desmond and the next MacCarthaigh Mór as he was illegitimate – an awful term to apply to any human. He was a smart man and he knew this, so he decided to bide his time before taking what was rightfully his, with or without a fight.

Rather than have his title and lands pass directly to the English Crown, his father tried to look for alternatives: arranging for his last remaining legal child, a daughter by the name of Ellen, to be married to Florence MacCarthaigh of the loyalist house of Carbery. In this way, the lands and titles would be protected within the clan, or so he thought. Seeing this was of no great advantage to their own ends, the Crown objected to the union, and for their insolence Ellen and Florence found themselves on an all-paid trip to Cork Gaol.

In the closing years of the sixteenth century, The MacCarthaigh Mór had finally passed away without any solution to the succession of his clan. Shortly after the death of his father, Dan returned from his hiding place in the remote bogs of Kerry to declare himself King of Desmond and The MacCarthaigh Mór. This was a direct challenge to the English, but also came with great rapture among the MacCarthaigh clan. He was immediately accepted and recognised by The O'Neill, who himself recently threw off the yoke of the imposed title of Earl of Tyrone.

But little did Dan know that Florence MacCarthaigh was conspiring with the English behind his back to steal the lands of The MacCarthaigh Mór. He had been promised the lands and titles by the Crown if he had Dan bumped off, and this is what he agreed to do.

As controversial then as it would be today, Dan and Florence went to meet with The O'Neill in March of 1600 to discuss matters, and under duress Florence was appointed as the new King and Chief – in effect removing Dan from his position. Karma got him in the end and he spent some more time in the Tower of London, around forty years, give or take a day or two.

Dan was once again crowned King of Desmond and The MacCarthaigh Mór, and he set about acquiring help from Spain to banish the invaders once and for all. Unfortunately, this help was hopelessly inadequate and they had to face the English at the Battle of Kinsale with insufficient numbers. This led to a cruel defeat and ultimately to the Flight of the Earls and the destruction of the old Gaelic order.

Dan was allowed keep his title for the rest of his days and also to sit in his ancestral home of Castlelough Castle, entertaining by day and sleeping in his feather bed by night. He was well known for the kindness of his hospitality, his weakness for fine ladies and for his enjoyment of a good drink.

He was buried in Muckross Abbey, where he remains to this day, but it is said that he arises every night to go for a stroll on the lake and then back to his slumber – but not before slipping into one of the local hostelries for a quick nightcap.

EOGHAN RUADH Ó SÚILLEABHÁIN

Eoghan (anglicised as Owen Roe O'Sullivan) was one of the last great Gaelic poets and one of the four famous Kerry Irish-speaking poets. He was largely unknown outside the Gaeilge-speaking regions of Ireland until the beginning of the twentieth century, although among Irish speakers his poems were well loved and there were many stories about his exploits.

Ireland's first president (and scholar) Douglas Hyde wrote briefly about him in 1903, and Daniel Corkery devoted a whole chapter to Eoghan in his 1924 book *Hidden Ireland*; taking much from an earlier work by Fr Patrick Dinneen. By all accounts, Eoghan was a hugely talented poet, ignored by the English but beloved even in his own time by the Irish, referred to as *Eoghan an Bhéil Bhinn*, or Owen of the Sweet Mouth. Unfortunately, he was also a rather reckless man, womaniser, drinker and 'wastrel', who greatly squandered his abilities.

Eoghan was born in 1748 at Gneeveguilla in east Kerry, in one of the few areas of Ireland still under the control of a native Irish chieftain – in this case MacCarthy Mór, who supported one of the last bardic schools of Ireland. It was here that Eoghan learned his craft; studying poetry in his own language as well as learning Greek, Latin, English and mathematics. Eoghan opened his own school at the age of 18, but an unfortunate incident, probably involving a woman, damaged his reputation and forced him to close down.

Red-headed Eoghan was highly intelligent, witty and charming, but this did him little good professionally – with the anti-Catholic penal laws being in full sway, finding substantive work was near enough impossible. With few prospects and no patronage for his vocation, Eoghan became a *spailpín* (itinerant labourer), drifting from place to place. By a stroke of luck he managed to secure teaching work for the Irish-speaking Nagle family in Fermoy.

When a servant needed a letter written to the master of the house, Eoghan volunteered to do so and not only wrote it in Irish but in English, Greek and Latin. The master was so impressed that Eoghan was immediately employed to teach the Nagle children but his luck was not to last long. After getting a woman of the house pregnant (some say Mrs Nagle), he was unceremoniously thrown out at gunpoint. Eoghan then found himself joining the British Navy, possibly at the hands of a press gang, and end up fighting in the West Indies. After a great victory against the French he wrote a poem for Admiral Sir George Rodney, which would have earned him a promotion had he not cheekily asked to be let go instead. He served in England for a time before apparently securing a medical discharge by ulcerating his shin with spearwort, after which he returned to Kerry and opened another school at Knocknagree Cross, near Rathmore on the Cork/Kerry border.

Eoghan supposedly gained some patronage from the Irish Cronin family, but the poet got into an unfortunate drunken brawl with one of Colonel Cronin's servants who he had satirised, leading to Eoghan being struck on the head with some iron tongs. He died of a fever a few days later, while still writing; the last lines he wrote appearing at the memorial for him in Knocknagree:

Sin é file go fann, nuair thuiteann an peann as a láimh.
(Weak indeed is the poet, when the pen falls from his hand.)

Apparently, a beautiful young woman was asked to lie down on the bed next to him to make sure that he was actually dead. Eoghan was buried at Muckross Abbey in 1784, just 35 years old. It's thought none of his works were written down in his lifetime, but were retained orally as songs by the people who delighted in his poetry. Fortunately, much of it was recorded later, some of which has been translated into English.

Some of the stories of his ribald life survive, demonstrating both his wit and notorious bad behaviour. On one occasion, Eoghan was sitting by the kitchen fire at a house where a priest was secretly hearing confessions, when a well-off farmer came in. The priest asked Eoghan to give up his chair for the farmer. Being somewhat hungover from a night's drinking he struggled to get up, cursing at the priest, and threw himself down on the pile of turf in the corner. After taking the confessions the priest began the Mass, but noticing that Eoghan hadn't stirred from the pile of turf he reprimanded him, to which Eoghan merely replied with a satirical poem in Irish despite his sore head. The priest suddenly realised who he had been speaking to and went over to shake him by the hand.

Eoghan had a reputation as a bit of a philanderer; it was said of him that if he threw a coin over a fence it would more than likely land on one of his illegitimate children. One day a young boy met Eoghan on the road and he spoke to him for a while. Then he gave the boy a penny, telling him that the next time he saw him he would give him a shilling. The sharp young fellow hopped over the ditch and ran over some fields, before rejoining the road further up from where Eoghan was walking. Shortly after, the lad came down the road towards Eoghan with a big grin.

'You said that you would give me a shilling the next time that you saw me,' he said.

'True enough,' replied Eoghan. 'Here is the shilling, and another for your intelligence. You must be one of my own.'

Another time, the poet was passing a priest's house with a friend and there was a grand smell of cooking salmon coming from the house. The two of them were hungry and the friend said to Eoghan: 'It's a shame that the priest should have more than enough and we should go hungry.'

'I'll bet you that I can both eat the dinner with the priest and put him to shame,' replied Eoghan. The friend readily agreed to the wager.

Eoghan knocked at the door and asked if he could see the priest. After seeing his rather bedraggled state, the housekeeper said, 'He is just sitting down to his dinner, and he said that he was not to be disturbed.'

'But it is a very important matter,' said Eoghan. 'Go up to him and tell him that I have a troubled mind, and that I want to know what a man should do if he has found money.'

When she returned she let him into the house, but said to him: 'The priest says that if you wait until he has his dinner finished, he will answer your question. He also told me to give you this herring,' said she, putting a pathetically tiny herring before him. Eoghan whipped up the wee herring and he whispered to it, then putting its mouth to his ear he listened. After watching him do this, the housekeeper went up to the priest again and told him he was 'not the full shilling'.

'Ask him what he is doing, and why is he doing it,' said the priest and so down went the housekeeper again.

'I had a brother who travelled abroad, and I was just asking the herring if he had any news of him,' replied Eoghan.

When the housekeeper told this to the priest, he thought that Eoghan must be a simpleton and he'd soon relieve him of the found money.

'Send him up to me,' he told the housekeeper with relish.

'You say that you can understand the language of fishes,' the priest asked of Eoghan.

'Yes,' he replied.

'I had a brother, too, who travelled abroad. Could you get news of him for me from your fishy friend there?' asked the priest.

'You had better ask that of the big salmon there,' answered Eoghan. 'He is a much bigger and stronger fish, and more used to priests and their like than this humble herring.'

'You are a good deal smarter man than I took you to be,' said the priest, realising that getting hold of the found money might not be so easy after all. 'You'd better join me and eat the salmon,' he said, thinking it might soften him up somewhat. After finishing the fish, the priest offered Eoghan a drink of punch, which he gulped down.

After a few more glasses of punch the priest asked, 'So you have a troubled mind about some found money?'

'Indeed I do,' replied Owen.

'Now how much money would it be that you found?' asked the priest.

'Only a penny,' said Owen. 'I was just wondering what would be the case if I really did find money.'

The poor priest nearly choked on his punch. Eoghan had won his bet and got a fine dinner out of it too, at the priest's expense.

The Pharaoh's daughter

Many moons ago, when the world was young, there lived a princess in a distant land far from Ireland. Her name was Scotia and she was the daughter of a powerful pharaoh, who had all of Egypt under his control.

The pharaoh found himself embroiled in a petty battle with the nation of Ethiopia and, given their superior military might, he knew that he was hopelessly outnumbered. One of his closest allies, a chieftain by the name of Míl, offered the assistance of his troops to his old friend in his time of need. The two armies joined forces and easily overwhelmed the Ethiopian military. Success was theirs and as a sign of his gratitude, the pharaoh presented his only daughter in marriage to Míl. An odd thank-you gift, you might think, but this was quite the done thing back in those days. Much to the relief of Scotia, Míl was a bit of alright in the looks and personality department, and so they soon fell in love.

Míl was also a bit of a warmonger and his council agreed that their next raid would be of the distant land of the Ciar in south-west Ireland. On the day of departure, he kissed his wife goodbye and set off with his fellow Mílesians in their warships. Scotia thought it best to wait and tell her husband when he returned that she was carrying the fruit of their love in her womb.

The voyage was long and tough, but eventually they landed at a mysterious place full of mighty trees and lashed by the

Elena Danaan

raging seas. It was cold, wet and dull in this land, not like the sunny shores they had left. They ran their ships up onto the beach and headed inland towards Tara, to challenge the status quo and see what they could take for themselves. They chopped their way through the thick undergrowth and suddenly heard the rustling of leaves and banging of drums all around them. The sounds echoed behind them, in front of them, and above them, but they could not tell exactly from where it was coming. Then they heard the roaring cries of men and women on the air, but could only see the faint glimpse of shadowy figures leaping from branch to branch, high up in the canopies. They knew that they were surrounded and the uneasiness grew in them. They became confused, disorientated and, for the first time, frightened. Their only option, Míl thought, was to head for a clearing in the trees ahead of them.

The men ran with all their might in search of refuge, but on getting to the clearing realised that it was a small open fort. In the centre of the fort was a throne made of whale bones, and in the throne sat a stout, half-naked man who was painted from head to toe in blue paint.

'I am the chieftain of the Tuatha Dé Danann, the blessed people of the Goddess Danu,' he said. 'You have blasphemed her and offended us with your presence here.'

With this, countless people, all painted blue, swung down from the trees clutching vines of ivy and surrounded the Mílesians. They were taken to a large pit that held many starving bears and they were thrown to their deaths.

The news of what had happened reached Scotia, now Queen of the Mílesians, and she was heartbroken. Her emotions went from overwhelming grief to overwhelming anger.

'I will avenge the death of my beloved Míl and the honour of the Mílesians!' she screamed. Her rage fuelled her to gather the remaining soldiers in the tribe and, with the help of her father's men, set out to the land of Ciar seeking retribution.

They arrived on the shores of Ireland and saw the ships left by their comrades on the beach. They followed the same path cut through the forest, but instead of heading for the fort clearing they turned off and stood at the top of the valley at Sliabh Mish and waited for the Tuatha Dé Danann to come. A great battle ensued shortly thereafter, but as the Mílesians had the higher ground, victory was easily achieved. Acknowledging the superiority of the Mílesians, a truce was declared for three days while the two peoples agreed to divide the entire land. Below ground would go to the Tuatha Dé Danann, who became the Sídhe, and above ground would go to the Mílesians, who became the Gael.

The pregnant Scotia rode up to a ridge at the edge of Sliabh Mish to wave her flag in declaration of the victory of the sons of Míl, but in a cruel turn of fate her horse bucked when the corner of the flag struck it in the eye, and Scotia was thrown off and down into the base of the valley. Both she and her unborn child succumbed to their wounds on the spot and they were buried there under a cairn of stones. The valley became known as Glen Scoithín, which means 'Valley of the Little Flower', and Scotia's grave can be seen there to this day.

THE DEATH OF FIONN MACCUMHAILL

Fionn MacCumhaill was no ordinary giant. He was a man of epic proportions, and of all the men and beasts in the land, he was the biggest and strongest. Said to stand at a whopping 52½ feet tall, Fionn could lift whole towns in his enormous hands and his voice could be heard from Antrim to Kerry, even as far away as the mighty kingdom of the Isle of Man. He led a full and eventful life of mischief, bravery and adventure, from the shaping of Ireland's coastline to the fighting of spirits, from battling other giants to leading the High King's private army as its Commander-in-Chief.

It was in the woods of Lyracrumpane, on the slopes of the Stack's Mountains, that Fionn was out hunting with the Fianna. They were in pursuit of a mighty elk that they had tracked for some distance from the south. The elk showed apparent unending stamina, as did Fionn, who was leading the charge.

Elena Danaan

They reached a gorge, known these days as Gleann na Léime (translating into English as Valley of the Leap), at the far northern end of the Stack's range. The elk, clearly familiar with the terrain, took a narrow path down one side of the gorge and up the other, with the Fianna following the route it had taken.

Fionn, being the fearless man he was, took a running jump and leapt high in the air and sailed effortlessly over the gorge. His men gasped in awe as their leader and hero soared high above them. Fionn grabbed onto the rushes that grew on the far edge of the gorge and pulled himself back up onto solid ground. He then took off and continued the chase in the direction of the beast, gaining ground on it all the time. Suddenly the elk slipped on a muddy patch and this was the moment that Fionn needed. He grabbed the beast by the antlers and, whispering a prayer of thanksgiving into its ear, he honourably took its life.

The Fianna caught up with Fionn and helped butcher the animal where it lay, then began retracing their footsteps back in the direction of their fort, where they planned to have a mighty feast that night.

The men were commenting on the merits of the mighty jump performed by Fionn and how impressive it was, but there was someone in the group who did not believe that Fionn's jump was all that fantastic. News of the doubter spread through the group and reached the ears of their leader.

Not wanting to be outdone, Fionn said to the doubter, 'Master Kiernan, if my efforts offended your eyes, perhaps you could show us how you impress your fellow man.'

Kiernan asked for room and ran to the gorge, taking a huge jump over to the other side, and even performing a somersault halfway over. The men applauded.

Thinking that there should not be anyone of his equal or greater within the ranks of the Fianna, Fionn said, 'Impressive, Master Kiernan, but can you perform the act backwards?' With that, Fionn ran to the edge of the gorge and turned his body backwards before jumping. It was a strong start, but attempting such a feat was just foolish and he barely reached half the distance as before. He plunged over 200 feet to his death and such was the horrific nature of his fall that his head was cleanly severed from his body and rolled to a place known today as Rockfield.

His beloved friends buried his head where it lay and marked its location with a large rock, which can still be seen to this day. Such was the force of the fall, that Fionn's footprint was permanently marked upon a sandstone rock at the base of the glen, which is also still visible. His body was taken and 200 yards to the east and buried at the entrance to the glen, marked by two flagstones.

The following poem was gathered from Pádhruigh Ó Muircheartaigh, during the Schools Folklore Commission in the 1930s, and we are blessed to have it here. It is thought that Pádhruigh himself composed this gem:

Some bards sing the praises of Old Ireland,
Of its glens, and dales, and vales.
Of old historic places,
Where lie the leaders of our race.
But there is a spot therein,
That just seems clear to all.
Where lies Fionn MacCumhaill,
The leader of the Fianna all.

Just visit this spot in Kerry,
And see for yourself today.
The leap of the fearless and mighty,
In the days long passed away.
Hush! Listen! The wind you will hear,
Whistling a charge o'er the grave where the hero is laid.

Be it Autumn-time when you visit the place,
When all nature is in decay.
There, you will see that the bloom of the wild flower,
Is still fresh and fair.
Here, little birds sing their mellow songs always,
The falcon too and raven old do pay winged homage pay.

All seen and conscious of the fact that here lies Fionn,
The once might of Inis Fáil.

THE WHITE BOYS AND THE GABHA BEAG

The White Boys were a violent movement of men who organised themselves into units back in eighteenth-century Ireland, based around the southern counties of Kerry, Cork, Waterford and Tipperary. Their main aim was to defend the rights of the tenant farmers who were constantly being harassed and exploited by landlords with excessive rents and unfair evictions, and also by the Church who piled hefty priests' tithes on the already burdened people.

The men were collectively known as 'the White Boys' because of the white smock tunics that they wore during their regular secret conferences and nightly raids. They swore allegiance to their mythical queen, Sadhbh Amhaltach, who represented the land of Ireland, with the Irish people being her children. The White Boys were also given the name 'Levellers' by the authorities due to their penchant of levelling the ditches, hedges, walls and fences that had been erected on common lands on the orders of the landlords.

During the 1740s and 1750s, landlords began to realise that owning clear pasture land for grazing was more lucrative and less troublesome than having their land tenanted by the peasantry. They began the slow but determined process of seizing farms, evicting the locals, and enclosing the commonages so that they could replace the people with cows and sheep, to fatten the animals and also their bank balances.

The people knew that this was not right, so they came together to form the White Boys, who would use violent means to defend the defenceless. They would ride out at night blowing horns and shooting their guns into the air as they went, sending shivers down the backs of many a landlord and landlord's agent. They employed a number of methods to destroy all manner of enclosures in a very real effort at freeing the commonages, but they also engaged in a campaign of fearmongering wherein they would erect gallows in front of the grand houses, dig empty graves at their entrances, or leave coffins with their names engraved on the lids. All of this would ensure that the ascendancy knew that they were not to be messed with, and God help any man who tried to get in the way of them while they were at work, for he would not usually live to see another day.

One such White Boy, a rugged blacksmith by the name of James Nolan, was put to death for his part in the attempted murder of a local landlord. Nolan was a short man, with a thick beard and long matted hair. He was known all around as the Gabha Beag, or the short blacksmith, and his deeds became the stuff of legend.

Nolan was given orders to go and shoot one particular landlord as he returned from his offices in Listowel. He lay in wait just inside the fence by the fort of Cremin's field in Ballydonohue in the darkness, until his intended target approached. What he was not expecting was to see the man being flanked by two armed policemen for his protection. The Gabha Beag fired a shot at the landlord, but his aim was off and he hit one of the policeman in the leg instead. He stood up to flee and ran *ar nós na gaoithe* down through the rushes in the field, but the remaining policeman saw him and ordered him to stop at once. Not surprisingly, Nolan failed to comply and the consequence of this was a gunshot that saw him hit the ground clutching his own leg. This certainly put a halt to his gallop.

He was taken and put into prison until his hearing was scheduled, and when he stood up in front of the magistrate no mercy was shown. He was sentenced to swing three times in the gallows of nearby Gunsborough.

When he returned to prison he asked for some clean clothes to be buried in, but the warder laughed at his request and said, 'If you can find someone to give you clean clothes, then I'll not object.' And so the Gabha Beag arranged with a fellow White Boy to send him some clothes the following day.

As the sun rose on Good Friday, 1808, the day of his execution, a brown paper package arrived for him tied up with bleached white twine. As he opened it, he saw a nice white smock tunic and black trousers, the uniform of the Whiteboys. Inside the collar of the tunic was an iron ring that he had fashioned himself in his forge, the purpose of which will soon become clear.

Dressed in his new clothes, the Gabha Beag was taken over to Gunsborough and up to the top of the scaffolding that housed the gallows. At the allotted moment, the executioner placed the noose around Nolan's neck and pulled the lever to release the trapdoor. He dropped down the vertical shaft and the executioner pulled him back up in readiness for his second drop, in line with his sentence. To the amazement of the executioner, Nolan was just as much alive as he was before! Little did the court's agent know, the iron ring inside his collar prevented the noose from cutting into his neck and choking him. He was hung a second time and came back up just as before, not a bother on him. He laughed in the face of the executioner, who was scratching his head in confusion. Nolan knew that if he survived the third hanging, he would be set free in line with the law.

Back in the prison, the warder mocked the Gabha Beag's friend, saying, 'Your friend will have been hung by now.'

The friend responded, 'The Gabha Beag will not die on this day.' Thinking that his friend will have been dropped three times and released by then, he told the warder about the iron ring in his tunic collar. The warder ran out of the prison and, jumping on his horse, headed for Gunsborough gallows. Just as they were about to drop the man a third and final time, they saw the warder riding furiously towards them from a distance and shouting for them to stop. As he reached them, he told them of the iron ring in the Gabha Beag's collar and when the executioner searched Nolan's tunic they found it. The Gabha Beag knew that he was done for and, as they re-tightened the noose and released the trapdoor, he blessed himself as he fell to his death.

A celebration of the life of James Nolan the Gabha Beag was held on the 200th anniversary of his death, and many of his descendants gathered around his anvil in thanksgiving for what he did for the poor tenant farmers and for Ireland.

THE CAPTURE OF SIR ROGER CASEMENT

McKenna's Fort at Rathcrihane, near Ardfert, is today better known as Casement's Fort – the place where Irish Revolutionary

Sir Roger Casement was captured and arrested on 21 April 1916.

Casement had been in Germany, recruiting for an Irish Brigade amongst Irish prisoners of war to fight in the intended uprising. After an offer of weaponry from the Germans, Casement returned to Ireland with his colleagues, Robert Monteith and Daniel Bailey, aboard the U-19 submarine in the early hours of 21 April at Banna Strand on the north side of Tralee Bay.

Meanwhile the ship SS *Libau*, disguised as the Norwegian vessel SS *Aud*, arrived in Tralee Bay on 20 April, three days earlier than expected – and with no arrangements for an earlier rendezvous. The German ship, carrying 20,000 rifles, a million rounds of ammunition, explosives and ten machine guns, attempted to escape but was blocked by British ships that had been alerted of a possible attempt to land arms. Not far from Cobh, the captain, Karl Spindler, scuttled the ship, sending his cargo to the bottom of the sea.

Casement had not felt well on the trip by submarine and shortly after the three landed at Banna Strand in a small boat, his comrades left him in order to go and find assistance. Daniel Bailey was captured, but Robert Monteith, with the help of one Fr Flaherty, escaped to Limerick and eventually to America. Unfortunately for the three men, they had been spotted at around 4 a.m. by Mary Gorman, who was up early to milk the cows and had seen them approaching from the direction of the sea. She quickly spread the news around the village and a John McCarthy went to investigate. At the beach he found a small abandoned boat and dispatched his nephew to inform the RIC at Ardfert. Sergeant Tom Hearne went with a constable to take a look and discovered three Mauser pistols, ammunition, signaling lamps, some maps and papers. The discovery immediately raised suspicions that this was no ordinary landing and, after taking the boat by horse and cart to the barracks, the police began to search the area for the three mysterious men.

After searching fields and calling at various houses, constable Bernard Reilly entered McKenna's Fort while his sergeant waited at the road smoking. A tall, smartly dressed man with a beard emerged from the shrubbery.

'What are you doing here?' Reilly asked him.

'Haven't I a right to be here?' the tall man replied, to which the constable explained that they were searching for strangers in the locality. The tall man replied that he was an Englishman and that his name was Richard Morton from Denham in Buckinghamshire. When asked how he came to be standing in an old Iron-Age fort in rural Kerry, the man explained that he was an author doing research for a book on the life of St Brendan. This rather implausible cover story was, in fact, coming from Sir Roger Casement, although the constable had no idea of who he was at this point.

Constable Reilly stated that Casement kept looking around and over his shoulder, which made him suspicious that he was not alone. He was also carrying a sword stick that he kept drawing in and out as he spoke. Reilly warned Casement that if he drew his sword he would fire the rifle that he was holding, although unknown to Casement the rifle was not actually loaded.

Sergeant Hearne arrived and asked more questions, before asking Casement to come with them to the police station to which he replied, 'I have no objection.' Accompanied only by constable Reilly in a pony and trap, Casement was taken to Allman's farmhouse where Mary Gorman identified him as one of the three men she had seen early in the morning.

The two RIC men walked Casement about a mile to the barracks in Ardfert, followed by a small group of locals and Collins, the young man who had driven the pony and trap. Collins later gave constable Reilly a piece of paper that Casement had dropped onto the road, which turned out to be writing in code that was later used as evidence at Casement's trial.

At around 1 p.m. Casement was taken by car to Tralee, beginning his imprisonment that ended with his infamous prosecution case and hanging for treason. Some time between 12 and 1 p.m., Austin Stack and Con Collins were spotted in a motorcar in the village of Ardfert, presumably hoping to rescue Casement, but unfortunately they were too late.

That evening, police searched McKenna Fort and found some packets of sausage sandwiches and three overcoats in the bushes. In the pocket of one of the coats was a train ticket from Berlin, which again was used as evidence against Casement. A memorial to Roger Casement now stands in the fort that bears his name, on the spot where he was captured.

The Wizard Prince of Ross Castle

Ross Castle is a fine example of a fifteenth-century Irish tower house, built for defence and dramatically set on the shores of Loch Léin. It is the ancestral seat of the sept of the Ó Donachadha Mór and in its heyday it withstood many a battle against Gael and foreigner alike, but its final undoing was the fulfilment of a pesky age-old prophecy, which declared that:

> *Ross may all assault disdain*
> *Till on Loch Léin strange ship shall sail.*

It was none other than Cromwell, who, being aware of the prophecy, knew that fulfilling it would have a much greater impact than mere brute force. He was right, the scallywag, and so he had gunships transported by oxen over land from Killorglin to the loch, where they were launched into its waters. This terrified all who saw them and, after a few cannon shots and nothing but a graze to the fabric of the building, the occupants of mighty castle surrendered.

Before the untimely destruction of the mighty fortress' spirit, it was home to a great and mysterious chieftain. The Ó Donachadha Mór was respected far and wide as a great warrior and magician, with vast knowledge of alchemy, dark arts, and the occult. From a young age, the chieftain practised incantations and made potions from the plants and herbs that grew around the lake. It was even said by some that he conversed with the devil himself.

As the chieftain grew older, as everybody eventually does, he developed a mortal fear of allowing nature take its course and ultimately becoming an old man. Given his vast experience in the old ways, he thought that he may be able to figure out a solution to his problem, and so he locked himself away for weeks on end in a remote part of the tower, high above where anybody would usually venture. Day and night he experimented with new potions and new spells in an effort to find a cure for what bothered him.

As the sun rose on May morning, a great commotion was heard over the dawn chorus. The Ó Donachadha Mór declared with great excitement from the chamber window that he had finally found the cure to ageing!

'My Lady! My Lady!' he exclaimed. 'Come hither, you must help me become young again!'

His woman came as she was bade, and upon reaching the top of the stairs knocked on the large wooden chamber door. Given the unpredictability of her man, she was understandably terrified and did not know what to expect. He opened the door and greeted his beloved with a wild, insane look in his eyes.

'I have found the cure, my lady, and I need you to read the incantation so that I might regain my youth!' he said. Knowing that he would accept nothing but her unwavering submission to his request, she reluctantly agreed, but he warned her with great fervour that she must recite exactly what is written, otherwise there may be a great punishment.

She took the large book and began to read what he had written. There were many strange words and symbols, as it was written in a strange language that she had never heard or spoken before. It was not the Gaeilge that they had grown up with. She pronounced the words as best she could, but it was soon clear to see that asking the lady to read such a spell in an otherworldly tongue was a foolish move.

A large storm quickly began to brew over the loch outside, and the waters became choppy and dangerous. The wind

picked up and ripped around the tower, pulling stone blocks out of the walls and crashing them into the torrent below. Although the lady continued to read, the vicious wind was so loud that she could not be heard anymore and the furniture was being shifted all around the chamber. Suddenly, a large dark hand of wind and rain reached in through the chamber window and snatched the Ó Donachadha Mór from where he stood. Shaking him violently, the hand pulled him out through the small window, shattering his mortal body and taking him downwards into the depths of the raging loch, never to be seen again.

It is said that had he remained in charge of the castle that it would never have fallen to the English, but it is also said that he lives to this day at the bottom of the loch in a large palace, ever preparing potions and reciting incantations. He visits his ancestral home every seven years on the anniversary of his watery incarceration.

Moll Kissane and Her Famous Shebeen

Moll's Gap is a famous section of the pass where the road splits between Sneem and Kenmare (part of the Ring of Kerry) that offers great views of the MacGillycuddy's Reeks and the Black Valley, which has been a major tourist attraction since Victorian times. Before the 1820s the entire stretch was just a rough track, but that all changed after construction began on a proper road, albeit a single lane.

Moll's Gap is named after Moll Kissane, who ran a shebeen (a small unlicensed pub) on a rocky plateau during the construction period, which ended in 1833 when the road became open for traffic and tourists.

Moll was famed for selling home-brewed poitín and whiskey to the construction workers, who had a difficult job creating the winding road that cuts through solid rock in many places. It was the only place for miles where anyone could get a drink and so no doubt was very popular.

Even though her shebeen is long gone, presumably due to lack of customers when the road was finished, the spot still bears her name. A café now stands there, although poitín is sadly no longer available for the weary traveller.

Moll's descendant, John Kissane, still lives in the area at Foardal a few kilometers away towards Killarney, where he runs Moll's Gap Sheep Farm where patrons can adopt a sheep.

Philip Céad Bó

Not far from the area of Cordal in the centre of the county lies the townland of Foyle Philip. Here, among the rugged and wild hills, there sits a small plot of ground with the crumbling remains of a little cottage. Many years ago, this little house was the chief abode of a man known far and wide as Philip Céad Bó, which means 'Philip of the Hundred Cows'. There is some confusion as to what his real name was, whether it was Philip Horan or Philip FitzGerald, but whichever is true, he was certainly infamously known by all and particularly feared by the wealthy across the land.

Philip had the difficult occupation of cattle rustler, and although he usually stole his bovine treasure from outside his own area, he was not beyond fleecing his own county man or woman when the mood took him. He was discerning in terms of who he would rob and so he ensured that only the wealthy would be the targets of his raids, and the poor would share in the spoils.

He would gather his men for a game of cards on a particular night and look over the maps he had stolen from the Ordnance Survey men working in the area. They would trawl through the papers and pick out the large houses with large farms, and from this they would decide where to hit.

The men would arise early on a Sunday and wait in the bushes until the farmer and his family left for Mass. As soon as they were in the clear, the men would run out, quickly round up the cattle and drive them across the land to the nearest boreen, where Philip would be waiting with a few wagons to load them on. He would then transport them back over into Kerry and release them into pre-set pens in some remote place. The day after every raid, he would slaughter a number of the cows and throw a great feast for the poor starving Irish of the

locality, and there would be great merriment and laughter for all. It was for this reason that he was the champion of the poor and they loved him so much.

One particular day, the local priest Fr Ignatius was on his rounds when he stopped by at the cottage of Philip.

'May I come in and have a word?' enquired the priest.

'*Tar anseo, a h-Athair.* Come in, father,' replied Philip. Now, I should say that Philip had very little sympathy or time for the clergy, for he believed that they were way up there in the ranks of corruption with the wealthy landowners and exploiters of the Irish.

He sat the priest down and they had a wee talk over a cup of tea.

'I have not seen you at Mass in such a very long time,' said the priest.

'That is true,' said Philip, 'but it is dinner time now, so let me prepare some nice veal for us to eat while we chat some more.' By the time the food was ready, the priest was weak with the hunger and his mouth was watering with the fine aroma and sight of roast veal and boiled vegetables.

As they sat down to eat he asked, 'Do tell me, sir, if in partaking in this meal I am consuming meat from a dishonest source.'

'It is as honest a meal as you will have ever ate, your Reverence,' said Philip, and so they both tucked in and had a fine night of conversation and banter.

Fr Ignatius left the house thinking that Philip was not at all as bad or dishonest as he is made out to be, and he strolled home with a smile on his face, thinking he had done his sacred duty in winning back a lost soul to the flock. His mind was very quickly to change, when he got home only to realise that his young pet cow was gone and the veal he ate not an hour previously was no doubt the same animal!

The priest fell to his knees and with clenched fists shouted, 'Curse you, Philip Céad Bó! Curse you!'

TOM CREAN, THE ANTARCTIC EXPLORER OF ANNASCAUL

Tom Crean was largely unknown a few decades ago, at least outside of County Kerry, but this unassuming and quiet Kerryman was a major figure in the exploration of Antarctica in the early 1900s.

Crean was born in 1877 to Catherine and Patrick Crean on their farm at Gurtuchrane, near to Annascaul on the Dingle Peninsula. As one of ten children he spent much of his time helping out on the farm, where they mostly grew potatoes and raised cattle. He learned to read and write at school, but is thought to have left at age 12 to help his father with the farm.

It has been suggested that, after an altercation with his father, Crean decided to leave and join the British Navy at the earliest opportunity. At age 15 he made his way to a Royal Navy station at Minard. Lying about his age, he managed to sign up in July of 1893. Tom, joining as a Boy 2nd class, served on a variety of different warships, proving himself to be hardworking and reliable, and was eventually promoted to petty officer 2nd class before being posted to New Zealand on the torpedo vessel *Ringarooma* in 1900. In December 1901, *Ringarooma* gave assistance to Robert Scott's ship *Discovery*.

Crean might well have disappeared into obscurity had not able seaman Harry Barker deserted the *Discovery* after striking a petty officer, leaving Scott a man short for his expedition. The 24-year-old Crean, having a reputation for being tough, was accepted by Scott when he volunteered as Barker's replacement, and so began the frozen adventures that would make him famous.

Tom was well-liked by his comrades and was considered one of the best at hauling sledges across the ice, which he did for a total of 149 days. In 1902, Crean was one of the twelve men who travelled further south than any humans had done before, but he returned to base camp while Scott, Shackleton and

Wilson pressed on before being forced to turn back, still some 500 miles from the South Pole.

Unfortunately, *Discovery* had become trapped in the ice that winter, and even in the summer of 1902-03 they were unable to break free. Crean and most of the crew stayed with the ship, while Shackleton left on a relief ship. During the two long years stuck in Antarctica, Crean survived falling through thin ice and other harsh experiences, before *Discovery* was finally freed in February 1904 and returned to Portsmouth.

Scott singled Crean out for his excellent work and recommended him for promotion to petty officer 1st class. Scott also requested that Crean, now a valuable and trusted colleague, join him in serving together on several ships over the next few years. Scott also chose Crean as one of the first to join him on his ship *Terra Nova* on his next attempt to conquer the Antarctic in 1910.

Surviving a violent hurricane near New Zealand, they made it to Antarctica in January 1911, racing to make the Pole ahead of Amundsen and his Norwegian team aboard the *Fram*.

With his previous experience, Crean was employed as an expert sledger and pony handler. He proved to be highly capable, managing to jump heroically across breaking ice and scale an ice wall when his tent was floating away in the night. He raised the alarm and saved his two colleagues Garrard and Bowers.

Crean joined Scott on the three legs of their ill-fated treck towards the South Pole. With 150 miles to go, Scott decided to send three of the men back. To Crean's great disappointment he was one of the three, despite his great strength, knowledge and experience.

He was not to know then that the polar party would never been seen alive again, and endured his own great struggle to bring Lashly and Evans to safety. By February 1912, Evans had scurvy and snow blindness and had to be pulled on the sled.

By 18 February it was clear that Evans might soon die. With 35 miles still to go and no more than two days rations,

Crean decided he would head for Hut Point alone to get help. Amazingly, he set out without a sleeping bag and only a chocolate bar and three biscuits to sustain him on an 18-hour walk through the harshest conditions on Earth. Totally exhausted, he managed the journey of over 30 miles, just escaping a terrible blizzard that would undoubtedly have finished him off. Crean's bravery led to Lashly and Evans being rescued by a dog team, and he was later awarded the Albert Medal and Polar Medal by King George and promoted to chief petty officer.

With the failure of Scott's party to return, Crean and his colleagues waited out the harsh winter before eleven of them set out in November 1912 to search for the bodies. Crean noticed an unusual protrusion in the snow, which turned out to be the tent inside which lay the frozen bodies of Scott, Wilson and Bowers. The team buried their comrades under a cairn of snow, placing a cross over it before returning with personal effects, journals and letters, which were brought back to England in 1913.

Despite several brushes with death and the tragic loss of his friend Scott, Crean was not deterred from further exploration. Ernest Shackleton well knew what an asset Crean would be after having worked with him on the *Discovery* expedition, and his heroic exploits on Scott's failed polar attempt. Shackleton selected Crean as his second officer in 1914 and he was one of six men for the attempt to cross the entire Antarctic via the South Pole.

In January 1915 their ship, *Endurance*, became surrounded by pack ice in the Weddell Sea off of West Antarctica. Crean had another close encounter with death during their attempts to free the ship, when he was almost crushed by a sudden movement of ice. The months dragged on as they failed to break free and by November the ship was so damaged that it began to sink.

Recovering what they could, the expedition decided to set up Camp Patience on the pack ice with their supplies and three lifeboats. Abandoning Shackleton's plan to cross the ice to Robertson Island, as the ice had begun to break up in the advancing Antarctic summer, they waited in hope that the drifting ice would carry them to Paulet Island, where there were emergency supplies. This plan failed and, as the ice continued to fracture, Crean took charge of one of the three vessels on their seven-day treacherous voyage to Elephant Island on the north-west tip of Antarctica.

Many of the men were ill with diarrhoea and seasickness, but Crean was one of four men still strong enough to find and set up a safe camp for the bedraggled party. Shackleton realised that help was unlikely to come and decided to modify one of the lifeboats for a hazardous voyage to South Georgia, 800 miles away. Initially he had planned to leave Crean at the camp, but included him in his six-man crew after Crean asked to come with him.

On Easter Monday, 1916, they departed on the largest lifeboat and endured a horrific two-week voyage, reaching South Georgia just as a hurricane threatened to dash them against the rocks of the island. Amazingly, the little boat survived two days in the hurricane before finally making land, minus its rudder, on 10 May. Unfortunately, the men had landed on the wrong side of the island and had no choice but to march across the hazardous terrain to the Stromness whaling station.

Crean, Shackleton and Worsley were the only three strong enough to make the crossing. Having already endured unbelievable hardship, the three managed the 37-hour march, which they did tied together with ropes, across glaciers and ravines in freezing weather. The other three men were soon rescued and attempts began to save their colleagues on Elephant Island.

Crean, Shackleton and Worsley returned on three different ships in four attempts before they were finally able to reach the twenty-two men trapped on Elephant Island. Amazingly, all of the men had survived the three-month wait while their comrades desperately tried again and again to save them.

Crean continued to serve in the navy during the First World War after their return, but he returned to Ireland briefly in 1917 to marry his childhood sweetheart Nell Herlihy in Annascaul.

Early in 1920, Shackleton asked Crean to join him once again on his ill-fated *Quest* expedition, which, due to a growing family, he fortunately turned down. Following a bad fall on his ship *Hecla*, he was given early retirement in March 1920, returning to Annascaul in the midst of the War of Independence.

Barely a month after Crean's return, his brother Cornelius, a sergeant in the RIC, was killed by the IRA in Cork. Tom, aware of the tense atmosphere in Kerry, kept quiet about his service in the Royal Navy and his three Antarctic expeditions, although he did call his pub The South Pole Inn, which he opened in 1927 and which remains open to this day.

Tom shunned the limelight, never spoke or wrote about his amazing exploits, and refused all request for interviews, even leaving the pub when people came looking to speak to him about his past.

In 1938 he was taken to Tralee hospital with appendicitis, but had to be transferred to Cork as no surgeon was available. The delay caused his appendix to burst and Tom died from the resulting infection on 27 July. He is buried in Ballynacourty cemetery, in the tomb he constructed himself.

St Senanus and the Lady

In 1808, Thomas Moore published the song 'St Senanus and the Lady' (set to the tune of 'The Brown Thorn') in the second volume of his *Irish Melodies*, immortalising a rather strange story that centres around Inis Cathaigh (Scattery Island), which lies between counties Kerry and Clare in the Shannon Estuary.

St Senan was born around 490 and became a missionary, visiting Europe before founding a bishopric that covered much of counties Clare, Limerick and a small part of north Kerry. It was on Inis Cathaigh that he established a famous monastery, which also became the seat of his bishopric. Although St Senan had formed two convents for nuns within his jurisdiction, he forbade women to come to Inis Cathaigh.

The legend, from which the famous song takes its name, refers to a female saint by the name of Cannera, who was the daughter of a chieftain named Cumania. She was renowned for her beauty, but early in life she consecrated herself to the service of God and became a hermitess. It is said that she had a great friend and adviser in St Mocomog, whose shrine was only a few miles away from her own on the Atlantic coast. Sailors were said to visit her shrine to pray for a safe return from the sea, and she is regarded as the patron saint of fishermen and seafarers.

The legend varies slightly – in one version she made her way to Inis Cathaigh to meet St Senan, as she had become old and knew her death was imminent. She had recently seen a vision of pillars of fire above churches all around Ireland, and the one at the abbey of St Senan was the tallest and brightest of all, prompting her pilgrimage. Having walked all the way to the shore of the Shannon, she requested to be rowed to the island, but no one dared take her. It is said that she simply walked across the water instead, but St Senan would still not admit her due to his edict that the monks of the island were required to stay away from women.

St Cannera, in an early plea for equal rights, debated with St Senan, pointing out that Jesus spent much of his time among women.

'Christ came to redeem women no less than to redeem men,' she said, and also quoted St Paul to him. Even so, he would not admit her to the island, but when she begged to receive communion and the last rites from him he agreed. St Senan warned her that she could not be buried on the island and that her grave would be washed away by the waves, to which she replied, 'That would be up to God.'

In alternative versions, an angel brings St Cannera to the island to meet St Senan before her death and sometimes St Cannera is described as St Senan's sister. In another version, it was her dying wish to be brought to Inis Cathaigh and be buried there.

Whichever version is correct, St Cannera was apparently buried by St Senan on the strand at low water mark. Her grave is said to still be there, albeit under the water. A flag known locally as *Leac na ban beannuighe* is displayed on the strand of Inis Cathaigh, and is thought to mark her last resting place. For some unknown reason, Moore's poem does not mention St Cannera by name and even implies that St Senan might have changed his mind had 'the lady' come in the light of morning and charmed him with a 'rosy smile'!

CHARLIE CHAPLIN'S LOVE AFFAIR WITH WATERVILLE

Waterville has become a popular tourist destination largely due to its associations with Charlie Chaplin, the biggest film star of the early twentieth century.

Chaplin and his family visited the town for many years, but it very nearly didn't happen at all. Chaplin had married controversially for the fourth time in 1943 to Oona O'Neill (daughter of the Irish-American Nobel-winning playwright Eugene O'Neill) and had eight of his eleven children with her. Having moved to Switzerland after Chaplin was refused re-entry to America in 1952, the family were a lot closer to Ireland where Oona had her ancestral roots. Walt Disney had visited Waterville on holiday in 1947 and it was he who recommended the small coastal town to Charlie.

The Chaplins arrived in Ireland for the first time in 1959 at Shannon Airport and Charlie drove them himself for the four- or five-hour journey to Waterville.

When they arrived at the Butler Arms Hotel in the height of summer, it was full up and the receptionist, Miss Lawless, apologised and sent them on their way. With Chaplin being 70 years old and looking nothing like his famous 'tramp' screen persona, she might well have dismissed the prospective guest's name as mere coincidence. Fortunately for Waterville, Miss Lawless mentioned to the owner that Charlie Chaplin had been in looking for rooms and had just left. Billy Huggard, the hotel owner, asked her which way they had gone and quickly jumped into his car and raced after them. Having caught up and managed to flag down the Chaplins' car, he explained that it was a mistake and that of course they had room for them. In fact, the quick thinking Billy didn't have any rooms available other than those belonging to himself and his own family.

The Chaplins returned to the Butler Arms and after quickly vacating their own rooms the Huggards were able to accommodate them for what turned out to be the first of many holidays.

The Chaplins stayed for a month and quickly fell in love with the area, so much so that they would come back every year at Easter and sometimes during the summer. They loved the peace and quiet and the fact that, despite Charlie's fame, they were treated like ordinary people. The children enjoyed horse riding, sand yachting and swimming, while Charlie liked to try his hand at fishing – although according to his daughter Geraldine he wasn't much good at it. In the evenings the Chaplins would join the other guests in the hotel to play snooker, table tennis, and generally have the craic with them.

Billy and Mary Huggard became good friends with the Chaplins over the years and even attended the wedding of the Chaplins' daughter Josephine at Corsier in Switzerland.

The Chaplin family continued to return to the Butler Arms every year until 1971, when they were featured in *This Week* magazine. By this time, the Chaplins had eight children and two nannies accompanying them. According to the article,

Charlie was considering locations in Kerry for filming of his final film project *The Freak*, which was to star his daughters Josephine and Victoria. However, despite having written a script, with both his daughters becoming married and his health deteriorating, Chaplin was never able to begin filming.

Charlie didn't return to Ireland, supposedly because of the Troubles that deterred many foreigners from visiting. Charlie died after suffering a stroke in 1977 at his home in Corsier-sur-Vevey, Switzerland, the town where he is also buried. Some of his descendants have houses in the Waterville area and are still in touch with the Hubbards to this day.

Charlie Chaplin's last visit to Waterville was nearly fifty years ago but he is far from forgotten – his name attracts thousands of visitors every year. The Butler Arms has the Charlie Chaplin Lounge named after their famous guest and, in 1998, a bronze life-size statue created by Alan Ryan Hall was unveiled near the sea. In 2011, with permission of the Chaplin estate, the town set up the Charlie Chaplin Comedy Film Festival in his honour, which takes place every year in August.

St Ó Trialliagh, the Missionary of Dysert

The little parish of Dysert, between Listowel town and Lixnaw and cut in half by the River Feale, was once called *Disert Ua Triallaigh*, meaning the hermitage of Saint Ó Trialliagh, who is patron saint of the parish.

Small fragments of the ruins of an old church lie in the parish, supposedly on the site of his original church, but it is thought that nothing now remains of the original building.

One of the last great Irish scholars Dubhaltach MacFhirbhisigh, writing in his own language, preserved what is the only known story about the saint in his magnum opus *Leabhar na nGenealach* (*Book of Genealogies*). The book, which he began in

1649, was completed in the late 1660s, just a few years before his unfortunate murder in a shop in Dun Flin, County Sligo.

Ó Trialliagh decided to leave his brothers and take up a holy life in service of God, and so secretly left his homestead on a journey that would bring him to settle in Disert, by the bank of the River Casan Ciarraighe. Unfortunately for Ó Trialliagh, his brothers discovered his plan and to stop him they bound him in an iron fetter that restricted his movements, thwarting his noble intentions – or did it?

Having done this to their brother, they took the key and threw it into the sea, ensuring that Ó Trialliagh could not escape. However, by a miracle, a salmon swallowed the key ensuring it would not be forever lost under the waves.

After some time Ó Trialliagh, still stuck in his fetter, managed to escape from Tinauley where the brothers lived. Finding a coracle, he managed to get in it and make his way to the sea. The little boat carried him, still with the fetter between his head and feet, around the west coast of Ireland and up rivers to eventually reach Dysert; all this time followed by the salmon that had swallowed the key.

Meanwhile his brothers, hearing nothing of his whereabouts.

A group of clerics, having heard of his plight, searched for the saintly Ó Trialliagh until they stumbled across him, still in his fetter at Dysert. The fetter could not be removed, but not long after finding the holy man a fisherman approached the clerics and they asked him go cast his net in the river for them. They said he would catch a net full of fish, but only to bring back three salmon and enough for himself.

Sure enough, the fisherman returned to them with three salmon. One was given to Ó Triallagh and when he cut open the belly of the salmon out fell the key to the fetter, which was duly unlocked with much rejoicing.

Ó Triallagh went on to become a well-known holy man and established his church there, giving the place its name. He is said to have gained the name Diclethe because he concealed himself while in flight from his brothers. The key was kept for a long time as a miraculous reliquary and was known by the name Glasán Ó Triallaigh, although this along with his church is now lost.

The Cailleach of the Dún

The figure of the Cailleach looms rather menacingly throughout Irish history; portrayed as an ancient goddess of the land, wisewoman healer, the veiled one or a wizened old hag.

She is perhaps most famous in Ireland as *An Cailleach Bhéara*, the hag of the Beara peninsula, but she is also referenced in many place names around Ireland, such as the megalithic sacred site of Loughcrew or formerly Sliabh Na Caillaigh in County Meath, which has its own legend about the Cailleach leaping from hill to hill and dropping the stones there from her apron. In later times she is often portrayed as a dark and frightening figure who brings the winter with her, disappearing again with the warmth of spring.

She features in many Irish legends such as the pursuit of Diarmuid and Gráinne, in which Fionn engages the magical help of the hag to bring about Diarmuid's demise, although she is also killed in the process.

She also features in the stories of Mad Sweeney and Niall of the Nine Hostages, as well as many other lesser-known ones.

The hag of Beara is also associated with Chorca Dhuibhne on the Dingle peninsula, where it is said that she was born. Her birthplace is given as An Teach Mór (the great house), supposedly the most westerly house in all of Ireland, at the end of the Dingle peninsula promontory. She is also given as the ancestor of clan Chorca Dhuibhne, after which the peninsula itself is named.

The following story is from Dunquin (Dún Chaoin), to the west of Dingle.

The Cailleach lived on the top of a mountain where the wind blew constantly; it was very hard to approach and no one did. There on top of the mountain she kept her great treasure.

One day, down in the village at the bottom of the mountain by the sea, the Cailleach rescued a live lobster from a lobster pot left at the front of a house and took it away home with her. When she got back to her hovel she stowed the lobster in her treasure box under her bed.

Another day, when the Cailleach was out, a brave (or maybe reckless) man climbed up the mountainside, leaning into the ferocious wind, intending to steal the Cailleach's treasure. He entered the tiny house, looked all around and finally under the bed, where he saw her old box. There was a hole in the side of the box just big enough to fit a fist through, so he reached his hand inside and felt around, looking for treasure. The lobster inside quickly clamped onto it and it would not let go, no matter how much he struggled. So, the man continued to lie on the floor with his hand stuck in the treasure box all day long, until he saw the sun beginning to set and the room gradually darkening. At this stage the Cailleach returned.

When the old woman saw the man lying there trapped she said, 'You have done well, lobster.' And with that she took up her hatchet for chopping firewood and chopped off the terri-fied man's head with a single blow!

CATHAL NA FRANCAIGH

Some 150 years ago in the parish of Duagh there was an occa-sional unwelcome visitor by the name of Cathal na Francaigh, which meant Cathal of the Rats, the reason for which will become clear. He was a peculiar kind of gentlemen, well known among the country folk as someone with a short fuse and who would set a charm or place a curse on someone for the littlest of causes.

Both he and his mode of transport were the oddest-looking sight you ever came across. He wore an old deerstalker hat on his head just like Sherlock Holmes, which covered long matted hair hanging down his back, and a long shaggy beard hanging down to his belly. He always sat on a little broken old cart, pulled by a white donkey with black spots, not unlike a Dalmatian.

He was oft seen on the Listowel to Cork Road, and although this was a main thoroughfare it remained quiet, as everybody avoided it for fear of coming by him on the road. If he called to someone's house looking for food or lodgings, no one dared to refuse for fear of being at the receiving end of his favourite charm, that of sending a plague of hungry black rats.

One day he called to the house of a man called Scannell for to seek some oats for his horse.

Scannell opened the door and said, 'I don't care an ounce for your horse, you'll not get a single grain from me!'

This was not a wise move, for Cathal responded, 'I'll take not just a grain, and more than just oats from you. You wait and see.'

Scannell went to bed with a belligerent but uneasy mind. He knew that he had made not the smartest of moves. He woke the following morning to find a hoard of rats raiding his outhouses and carrying off all his worldly goods – he even saw them making off with his prize heifer on their backs. He tried to shoo them away, but it had no effect. In no time, they were pulling up and throwing down the thatch from his roof and chewing on the support beams for the house. It was not long before the house had collapsed in on itself and in no more than one short day he was completely ruined, the poor craythur.

Now don't get me wrong – Cathal was not always so vengeful and he didn't always cause trouble, but he was selfish and did have an awfully short fuse.

On another occasion he was going through the village of Duagh in his little cart. He was minding his own business and playing his fiddle, as he often did, when all of a sudden the children playing in the local schoolyard came out and began throwing muck balls at Cathal and his poor donkey. Cathal's temperature and his temper rose to boiling point within seconds and he pulled the reins on his donkey and turned into the schoolyard. Out came the schoolmaster, looking to see what all the commotion was, only to be berated by Cathal. The schoolmaster was used to taking no nonsense and so ordered him out of the yard and back on to the road.

While on the road, Cathal roared at the schoolmaster, 'I will be on my way now, but will tell you now to expect every rat from every graveyard or lonely place in this parish paying you a visit on this night.'

The schoolmaster laughed off Cathal's threat and told him to be quick about being on his way.

The schoolmaster lived not far from the school, and when the bell rang to signal the end of the learning day he set off for home as he had done on many a day before. He looked forward to the nice pie that was waiting for him for his tea, but that went up in a puff of smoke as he rounded the corner and saw, to his amazement, that the thatched roof of his cottage was being ripped up and eaten by a massive hoard of large black rats. He ran inside to see what other damage was being done and saw that the rats were on the walls, on top of the presses, in the windows and even on the table eating up his lovely pie. He was terrified and didn't know what to do, so he hurried to the parish priest for some advice. The priest came to see the vermin for himself and so grave was the situation that he advised the teacher to ask Cathal in the nicest possible way to release his charm.

The following day, the schoolmaster went to look for Cathal and found him drinking in Brosna at the house of a man called Nolan. The schoolmaster apologised profusely and begged him to come back the next day and remove the rats, which he promised to do on the condition that they both share a drink together.

The next day came quickly and they both rode back into Duagh in Cathal's little donkey cart. Everyone was lining the street, watching to see what manner of charm he would use to fix the infestation. Cathal rode his little donkey into the garden of the schoolmaster's house and reached into his satchel. He pulled out his fiddle on which he played a most peculiar tune. As he did so, all the rats retreated from the house and left in military formation. He rode his donkey up the road and the vermin marched behind him until he reached the Glashamore River, where he stopped and ordered all the rats to disappear.

At once they all jumped into the river and vanished, and from that day to this not a single rat has been seen in the parish of Duagh.

Diarmuid and Gráinne

Many stories are told across the land of the plight of Diarmuid and Gráinne, and here and there throughout the country are places said to have various connections with them.

There is one such place in the townland of Kilconly South. It is at this place where Diarmuid and Gráinne are said to have slept while fleeing the jealous pursuit of the mighty Fionn MacCumhaill.

I should bring the story back a little bit and explain that Gráinne was not only the most beautiful woman in Ireland, but also the daughter of Cormac Mac Airt, the High King of all Ireland. She was pursued for romance by many of Ireland's rich, famous and most eligible men: chieftains, princes and kings alike. The mighty Fionn MacCumhaill even set his sights on the beauty and asked that she allow him to take her hand as his second wife.

The young lady accepted Fionn's proposal and the Fianna threw a grand banquet for them to celebrate the fantastic news of their leader and his new woman. On the very same evening of the celebration, while Fionn was dozing from too much food and too much mead, Gráinne became acquainted with one of his best generals, a fine strapping lad by the name of Diarmuid. Diarmuid was young and strong, unlike the ageing Fionn. Her heart began to thump uncontrollably, so much so that she thought it would jump right out of her chest! Little did she know at that time that Diarmuid was also experiencing the same sensation. They both knew at that very moment that they had fallen utterly and deeply in love, a love so strong and so rare that nothing could part them from that point forward.

Gráinne was prepared to do whatever was necessary to make Diarmuid hers and so she prepared a potion and slipped it into the big bowl of mead that sat at the end of the grand table in the banquet hall. It had the effect of making Fionn's men fall into a deep, but temporary, slumber.

Knowing that they did not have much time, the two lovers made their escape and set off to make a new life together. Just as they left the hall, Fionn awoke and saw the couple depart, and realising what was happening he flew into a blind rage. He let out a loud roar, stood up and turned over the table in anger, sending all the food and drink crashing everywhere. He roused the men and ordered them to prepare for the pursuit of the two traitors.

The two eloped and were chased all across the land, hiding and sleeping in all manner of nooks, crannies and caves. They were pursued by a furious Fionn, with his soothsayer and army of men. Diarmuid was very smart, and wherever they slept he played a trick, so as to confuse the soothsayer. If they slept on the beach he would gather up heather from the mountains and they would make a bed from it, if they slept in the mountains he would gather up sand from the beach and make a bed from it. The soothsayer would tell Fionn what the couple slept on, so sending them off track.

After many years on the run, Gráinne became pregnant with Diarmuid's child, but fate was about to take a turn for the worst and one day while out in the wilderness, a giant boar confronted them. This was very bad news for Diarmuid, for legend had foretold that the only living creature that could harm him was a wild boar. The boar snorted, stamping his hooves on the ground, and suddenly charged at the couple. Diarmuid stepped out in front of his lady to protect her from the beast and was gored by one of his tusks. He yelped out in pain and drew his sword, slicing the animal's head from its body. He fell to the ground with the life being sucked from him. Gráinne could not believe what was happening. She knelt down, cradled her love's head in her arms and wept.

That was when Fionn and his men came upon the couple, and Gráinne begged him to cure Diarmuid with a drink of magic water from his cupped hands.

Fionn laughed heavily and spat on the ground, 'I'll not be saving any traitor on this day!'

His soldiers also begged Fionn to do something, as they knew that Diarmuid was a good man with a noble heart.

Finally, Fionn's son Oisín pulled out his sword and said, 'If you will not save Diarmuid from death, then it will be you that will join him on this day!'

On hearing this from his own son, Fionn reluctantly agreed to help – but by then it was too late and Diarmuid had died in the arms of his lover.

3

LOCAL CUSTOMS AND OLD KNOWLEDGE

LORE OF CERTAIN DAYS

Up until recently, throughout Ireland and particularly in Kerry, folklore was attached to days of the week and certain days of the year, which varied from district to district.

What was auspicious in one area might not be so favourable in another, although Monday seems to be have been considered universally unlucky! The details given here were collected in the 1930s.

Monday seems to be generally considered an unlucky day: ploughing, getting married, moving house, cutting hay, starting a job, and building a house are all not recommended. It was also thought unlucky to sow crops or any plants on Easter Monday; it was said they would not grow at all. Some farmers also believed that Friday was an unlucky day for sowing.

Hansel Monday was the first Monday of the year and it was thought if you received money on that day you would have good luck all year, the opposite being true if you paid out money.

Certain herbs had to be picked on Wednesdays after sundown, otherwise all the good would be gone out of them. A weaver would not put the new thread in a loom on any day but Wednesdays.

Thursday was often considered an unlucky day to move from one house to another, although not as bad as Monday. Friday, on the other hand, was seen as being unlucky to begin building a house by some but it was thought to be a good day to move house. People would not shoe a horse or an ass on a Friday, for fear that it would cause the person to get toothache. Some men also thought it unlucky to shave on a Friday.

Stonemasons and carpenters thought Saturday a bad day to begin building a house, believing it would bring them bad luck all year. Also, if a mason changed from building one house to another during Lent, it was thought to bring bad luck for the remainder of the year. Saturday was lucky for farmers; it was thought a good day to start ploughing. If a dressmaker started a job on a Saturday, they said it would never be finished: 'Any clothes cut on a Saturday are never finished' is an old saying.

There is a curious rhyme for the week, which does not include Sunday, perhaps because it was the holy day:

Monday for health,
Tuesday for wealth,
Wednesday for sorrow,
Thursday for losses,
Friday for crosses,
And Saturday for no luck at all.

It was thought very unlucky to wear a new suit of clothes, for the first time, at a funeral.

The third Thursday in March was thought to be an adventitious day for the planting of potatoes, although many people considered any date prior to St Patrick's Day or alternatively 20 April as fortunate. Spuds sown at a date later than this were thought to be not good and were called 'cuckoo potatoes'. It was said to be unlucky to sow potatoes after the cuckoo arrived. Cereal crops were to be planted before 22 April in order to be lucky, if they were planted after this they were called 'buckoo oats'.

The day when crosses were hung over doors was called the 'cross day' of the year, which was St Brigid's Day. These were put up in houses and animal stalls for protection and good luck. A small piece of cloth (Brigid's Mantle) is hung out in some households. A great many customs relating to good luck are attached to St Brigid's Day (1 February), some of which are still with us. Early April was called the 'days of the old tour'. This meant that if an old cow survived the bleakest days of March, it should survive the whole summer.

It was considered unlucky to pick flowers on May Eve. It was common to sprinkle holy water over animals on this occasion to protect them from fairies during Bealtaine. On St Martin's Night, 11 November, a hen or any other fowl is killed and its blood is sprinkled in the four corners of the house or sometimes on the outside walls. No wheels are turned on St Martin's Day in honour of St Martin of Tours who reputedly was tied to a wheel and pulled through the country.

On St Stephen's Day groups of young boys wearing masks of straw gathered together and went from house to house, singing the Wren Song. They collected money to bury a wren (caught earlier) and buy drink. The song went as follows:

The wren! The wren! The king of all birds,
On St Stephen's Day he was caught in the furze.
Although he is little his family is great,
Get up little lady and give us a treat.
Up with the kettle and down with the pan
Give us a penny to bury the wren.

Money collected was generally spent on drink. The wren boys are still to be found in Dingle town on St Stephen's Day.

CURES

The witches of *Macbeth*, stirring their large cauldron and chanting their spells with 'eye of newt and toe of frog', could well have been related to some of our own ancient and modern healers of the land. From healing mumps, sties, warts, head-aches and even worms, many of our superstitions and remedies do appear to be strange on the face of them – but who are we to balk at an ancient skill that has apparently worked for many, just because we don't understand it?

Herbal medicine in Ireland is a thread that refuses to be broken and is actually currently seeing a resurgence in interest, with new knowledge, learning and research showing that it is not all nonsense like so many would have us believe. Many of the myriad illnesses to which the human being may succumb respond to the healing powers of the plants that grow in the fields, bogs and meadows.

This botanical, sometimes faith-based medicine is the tra-ditional and indigenous medicine of the Irish. It is a knotted, tangled and almost-but-not-quite broken thread of a system that once cared well for Irish society until its displacement and dislodgement in the political turmoil of our history.

Included here are a number of cures that were (and some that continue to be) used by many Kerry locals over the centuries.

Dead Hand
The hand of a corpse was believed to be a cure for all diseases. Sick people were brought to a house where a corpse was laid out so that the hand could be laid on them.

Warts
The wart is a little lump of flesh that grows on the hands. If you meet a black slug when not expecting to meet it, pick up the snail and rub him to your wart. Then stick him on a thorn of a

sceach (poor little craythur). This treatment must be repeated twice a week, on a Tuesday and Thursday, using the same snail, and when he withers away so will the wart.

Burns
The candles used at funerals were also thought to have curative powers. The butts of the candles would be saved to cure burns.

Mumps
A person whose mother's surname has not been changed by marriage is supposed to be able to perform this cure for mumps: the person suffering from mumps has a halter put on him and is led to a stream by the curer. The curer then takes three drops of water, one after another, in his hand in honour of the Blessed Trinity and gives them to the person to drink. This is done for three days in succession and the mumps will be cured after this period.

Heartburn
A cure for heartburn was to chew briar leaves. A similar cure was to eat the tops of briars.

Whooping Cough
Milk an ass that is rearing a foal. The person who is suffering is to drink the milk and this will cure him.

Anxiety
Our ancestors believed that the clippings of the hair and nails of a child, tied in linen and placed under the afflicted person's bed, would cure convulsions and fretting.

Headache
A cure for a headache was to put vinegar on brown paper and put it to your forehead. The corner of the sheet used to wrap a corpse was also used to cure a headache or a swollen limb.

Another cure for headaches was the placing of a cloth on the forehead that had been left out on St Brigid's eve to receive her blessing as she passes over the land.

Elf-shot

Cattle are sometimes supposed to be elf-shot, an affliction caused by the arrows of the unseen. They get localised swollen limbs and refuse to eat anything, and, if not treated, they finally die.

The cure is made with a long briar which has rooted itself twice. The briar is measured three times round the body of the animal. During the measuring a particular rhyme – known only to the curer – is said. This is done each day until the measurement gets smaller and stops when the animal reaches its normal size. This cure is not handed down from one person to another. Anyone who knows the rhyme and gets the proper briar can make this cure.

CUSTOMS AT WEDDINGS, FUNERALS AND WAKES

Customs and traditions are as much a part of the Irish psyche as are music and dance.

Life and Love

Weddings are very happy occasions and can take place at any time of the year. There can, however, be a bit of an unusual rush around Shrove, just as there was in the olden times. June and September are said to be particularly unlucky months for nuptials, while the ceremonies are generally held on Mondays, Tuesdays or Wednesdays, as people are inclined to believe the old saying recounted earlier in 'Lore of Certain Days'. There is no mention of Sunday in the rhyme, so no one ever hears of a marriage on a Sunday.

Traditionally, as is still the case today, the bride wears:

Something old,
Something new,
Something borrowed,
Something blue.

Often times an old shoe was thrown after the wedding car to bring good luck.

A bride never returned to her own home until after the fourth Sunday in her new home and the newly married pair were not obliged to attend Mass on the first Sunday after their marriage.

Here is another old, and somewhat bizarre, saying:

Change the name,
But not the letter,
Marry for worse,
Not for better.

And an old rhyme regarding colours goes:

Married in blue,
Your lover is true.
Married in black,
You are sure to come back.
Married in white,
You have chosen right.
Married in grey,
You will go far away.
Married in brown,
You will live out of town.
Married in yellow,
You'll be ashamed of the fellow.
Married in green,
Ashamed to be seen.

Married in grey,
You will rue the day.

In olden times, an oaten cake was broken on the bride's head when she came home after the ceremony. When the bridal couple were returning from the chapel, someone would meet them with a bottle of whiskey, treat them, and then break the bottle.

Death and Mourning

On a more sombre note, when a person in the house died, all clocks were stopped and were not wound again until the corpse left the house.

Anyone who went to a wake would have brought a pipe full of tobacco home. Tobacco was supplied for the men and snuff for the women.

It was considered unlucky to leave a corpse alone, one should always have had company.

If a corpse was not quite stiff when being put in the coffin it was supposed to be a sign that another death would take place in the family before long.

The person who washed and laid out a person should also coffin them.

If the bed where the corpse was waked was at the back wall, it was belived that the coffin should be taken out by the back door. If near the front wall it should go by the front door.

The 'feet end' of the coffin should go out first, and when the funeral reached the graveyard the coffin was turned so that the head faced west.

Four people of the same name as the corpse took the remains from the house and again into the graveyard. The funeral went by the longest route to the graveyard and the relatives were warned not take any shortcut going home.

A person who met a funeral on the road was meant to walk back at least three steps and say a prayer.

SEANFHOCAIL - WISE OLD IRISH SAYINGS

The Irish have a wealth of strange and wonderful proverbs on old sayings. Many came down from the old Irish and simply translated while others are imports but ring true to life.

Below are a number of the local and more common ones.

Fools' names like fools' faces, always seen in public places.

The nearer to the church, the further from God.

Two heads are better than one.

A rolling stone gathers no moss.

Better wear out shoes than sheets.

He who slings mud is losing ground.

Take the world as it is, not as it ought to be.

A constant drop wears a hole in a stone.

Reading is to the mind what exercise is to the body.

Beware of a silent man and a dog that does not bark.

WEATHER LORE

Speaking about and dwelling on the weather, for better or worse, has always been a favourite pastime (some say obsession!) for many an Irish person; the Irish rarely being satisfied, as they are, with how it is outside at any given time. In the olden times, before scientific appliances were invented, people guessed weather conditions by the appearance of the atmosphere. People knew that the look of the sky, the direction of the wind, the behaviour of animals, birds and insects, and natural features all respond in their own way to changes in weather conditions.

Over the millennia, the Irish have devised a marvellous array of methods to predict the weather based on natural arrangements. These methods are many and varied, and are all sure signs which foretell changes in the climate. Here are but a few:

Those faced with a red sunset in summer know that this is a sign of fine, warm weather to come, while in winter it is regarded as a sure sign of frost.

A bright ring around the moon is looked upon as a sign of rain, while a clear sky and many twinkling stars foretell frost.

Those waking in the morning to a bright rainbow outside look upon this with great alarm as it is a sign of continuous rain; but a rainbow in the evening is not looked upon with any alarm as the spell of bad weather is not to continue.

The wind blowing from the east and south-east is a sign of good weather. The wind blowing from the north is a sign of cold weather, sometimes bringing frost and snow.

When the seagulls come inland it is a sign of storm. If the swallows fly high it is a sign of fine weather but if they fly low it is looked upon as a sure sign of rain. The robin is looked upon as being the best weather prophet of all: he becomes so bold as to come into the house to you, looking for something to eat at the approach of snow.

The sheep are also good weather prophets as they will move into the highlands at the approach of snow. They are afraid that the snow will fall down from the highlands and cover them.

The donkey usually turns his back to the wind at the approach of rain.

If the dust flies along the road it is a sign of rain.

The smoke from the farmhouse chimney ascending perpendicularly into the air is a sure sign of fine weather.

Despite this wealth of methods of foretelling the weather, we are still known for being notoriously bad at predicting the climate.

PISHOGUES OR PISEÓGAÍ

There are many forms of dark magic in many lands and *piseógaí* are Ireland's answer to the curse. They cover a multitude of scenarios and situations and, for the most part, can result in dark consequences befalling the person at the receiving end. They usually originate with the fairies, though they can also be set by people – usually someone with an axe to grind.

Piseógaí may be avoided in many cases by following certain rules in certain situations, although some cannot be so easily escaped, usually those set by jealous neighbours.

Here are but a few from Kerry:

You should not throw old water out after 8 o'clock at night, as you may drench the fairies on their travels.

Seeing one magpie is considered bad luck, although you can reverse it by saying, 'Bad luck to you, good luck to me. Fly away magpie and bring your comrade to me.'

The last person to leave the church following a funeral would be the next one to die.

Whoever takes a child home from their baptism must enter by the front door and leave by the back door.

If you milk someone's cow on All Hallows' Eve, you will have all of their produce for the following year.

Be wary of finding eggs in your hay, for they are placed there by persons wishing you ill will.

If you crawl under a briar with the two ends growing from the ground, you give your body and soul to the devil.

The tongs should be kept on the right-hand side of the hearth at night to keep the fairies away while you sleep.

Children will grow no further if they put a spade or shovel on their shoulder inside the house.

Don't cut a baby's nails or you'll make a robber of it.

A candle should never be lit during daylight or it's a sure sign of a dark year ahead.

Holy water should only be disposed of in the back of the fire.

If you meet a hedgehog on the road to a fair, you should turn around and return home for you will not sell any of your produce on that day.

RIDDLES

Who doesn't like a good riddle now and again? Being masters of language, the Irish love a good brain teaser and tongue twister. Below are a few local favourites:

What goes up when the rain comes down?

An umbrella.

What is the difference between a schoolmaster and a post office clerk?

One licks with a stick and the other sticks with a lick.

What walks with its head down?

A nail in your boot.

What is the difference between a hill and a fill?

One is hard to go up and the other hard to get down.

What is the difference between an engine driver and a schoolmaster?

One minds the train and the other trains the minds.

FOLKLORE OF FIRE

The fireplace is still important in Irish homes, but in days gone by it was the centre of the home: where people cooked and ate, heated water for washing as well as making tea. It was where people sat to keep warm, with the fire often kept alive day and night, and where people talked and sang – so it's no wonder that the fire itself became part of Irish lore.

Some folk beliefs related to the fire and hearth were as follows:

If a sod (of turf) faced out of the fire it was a sign of a visitor coming to the house. If that sod was smoking it was a sign that it would be a male visitor, smoking a pipe.

For good luck, one should always put the tongs on the right side of the fire. To avoid back luck, one should never bring fire across water, for instance carrying embers over a kettle or pot of water.

When going to bed at night it was said you should rake the fire, bring in a bucket of water and leave the tongs on the right side of the fire. This was to placate the 'good people' (*sidhé*), if they should come into the house.

It was considered very bad luck to burn elder in the fire. This is because elder is the female fairy tree. There was also a good practical reason for this – due to the nodules in the wood, the branches trap moisture and have a tendency to explode.

If a spark jumped out of the fire, it was a sign that money would come your way. If you threw the skins of an onion into the fire it was said to help you get money.

It was bad luck to take a coal out of the fire while a woman was making butter; neither should you take a coal out of the fire on a Monday. In the old days, no one was supposed to take a coal from the fire out of the house.

One was warned never to kindle the fire unless everyone was in the house. It was advised never to throw breadcrumbs nor milk into the fire. It was thought a bad idea to have one's fortune read by the fire and also bad to wash your feet near it.

If making a fire at night one should not throw any ashes on the fire. One shouldn't make a fire late at night, as the souls of the departed may want to take the heat of the fire.

It was advisable not to leave clothes to dry by the fire at night and it was also considered unlucky to dry anything written, such as a letter, by the fire.

4

ANCIENT PLACES AND FABLED SPACES

THE CITY AND THE PAPS OF ANU

Not far from Shrone Lake, at the foot of the two breast-like mountains (the Paps of Anu), lies what is referred to locally as 'The City' or Cathair Crobh Dearg, which means 'enclosure of the red claw.' This ancient site is the closest fort to the Paps, which are named after the Tuatha Dé Danann Earth Goddess, Anu or Danu. This leads many to believe that it may be one of the first settlements of the Tuatha Dé Danann, although excavations so far prove settlement only as far back as perhaps 60 BC.

However old it really is, The City was an important walled site, with a significant standing stone thought to have been carved with ogham writing that has since worn away. There are the remains of a dolmen there, now almost completely hidden, as well as a more modern stone altar, the famed holy well and the decaying remains of two tiny houses that were occupied well into the twentieth century.

The stone at the centre of the site is said to have had the top broken off by some ancient enemy, but no one knows when or by whom.

Folklore associates The City with one of an ancient triad of war goddesses, perhaps later known as St Craobh Dearg, reputedly one of three sister saints. The site has also been linked with the Red Branch Knights of Irish mythology, St Brendan, and the burial of an unknown Irish chieftain.

One old story tells of two giants who fought a battle on the Paps of Anu, overlooking The City, during which one took up a big boulder and flung it at his enemy with great force. His aim was pretty poor and he completely missed his foe, with the stone landing many miles away in the townland of Gallán.

The City remained a place of pilgrimage into the middle of the last century, with a 'pattern' held from May Day until 12 May. People travelled from all over Kerry, Cork and Limerick counties to visit the well, which was reputed to have great healing properties for those who were ill, lame or blind. In addition, farmers from the surrounding area brought their livestock to be blessed, driving them in a circle around the site before proceeding to the well.

There is a legend told of a thief who stole a fine ox on May night, when the cattle were brought to the site to be blessed there, but he was punished in divine retribution by God and tied to a stone on the pathway across the mountains from The City to Clydagh. The impressions of the robber's foot, his stick and the ox's hoofprint were said to be left in the stone some 200 metres from Shrone Lake, visible to passers-by at a place called Rían na Dabh.

According to some, the tradition of this pilgrimage dates back to the tenth century, although others suggest much later. It is said that, for a time in the eighteenth century, the well was closed down by a local 'tyrant' named Cronin, although the tradition was re-established into modern times.

The people performed 'rounds' at The City, going many times around both the outside and inside of the enclosure, saying prayers before going to the well. At the well pilgrims waited to take jars of water, to drink it or put it on themselves, sometimes leaving money at the old altar or in the well. Even today, the local people of Shrone village and nearby Rathmore celebrate mass at The City on 1 May, and the site is visited by tourists, Christians and Pagans throughout the year.

The Mountain Stronghold of Cú Roí

Cú Roí MacDáire was the King of Munster and a giant in the world of magic and sorcery. He had his chief fort high above the cliffs and ledges of the great Sliabh Mish mountain range, but he was rarely seen there due to his penchant for travelling the world. His ferocious thirst for knowledge led him to every land known and unknown on the earth, and so often was he away that it is said he did not eat from the fruits of Ireland from the time of his childhood until his death.

Such was the concern of the king for the safety of his people back on Sliabh Mish that he would place a charm on the fort every evening. Before retiring for the night, he would sit cross-legged in deep meditation and chant a spell in a very old tongue. This spell would cause his fort back in Ireland to spin around fast like a millwheel from dusk to dawn, with the result that the entrances were hidden and nobody and nothing could find a way in from the outside.

The mighty Ulsterman Cú Chulainn of the Red Branch was visiting a friend across the water in fair Cymru, when he met Cú Roí drinking in one of the dark and damp hostelries there. He bade Cú Chulainn to sit and join him for a drink and they chatted for some time about their land and peoples. As the bartender slammed down two more jugs of ale on the table, Cú Roí knew that his companion was making small talk and had something he really wanted to discuss.

'Spit it out, man!' snapped Cú Roí in anger. 'I don't have all day for this nonsense!'

'I wish to go on a raid of a hidden land beyond the great veil and would like you to be part of our attacking party. It will be a dangerous raid, but for your help you will have first choice in the spoils of this raid,' Cú Chulainn said.

When the king heard of the potential rewards, he eagerly agreed and set about making plans for the attack.

They met at the entrance to the otherworld near Cruacháin, and one by one they filed down through. Many were slaughtered in the calamity that followed, but through Cú Roí's bravery they were triumphant, and they carried off Midir's daughter Blathnaid, his cauldron of plenty and his magical cows.

As they emerged on the other side of the veil, Cú Roí placed his hand on Blathnaid.

'This will be my payment, and I shall take her as my wife,' he said. But the Ulstermen said that he could have nothing and they all began to laugh at him. In anger, Cú Roí picked up all the spoils and began to walk out, when Cú Chulainn stood up and placed his open hand on Cú Roí's chest. Cú Roí lifted him up with one hand and flung him back down to the ground with such force that he found himself buried up to his armpits. If this were not undignified enough, Cú Roí took his sword and sliced the locks from Cú Chulainn's head – a grave insult to any knight of the Red Branch. No other knight tried to intervene and Cú Roí left unassaulted.

Cú Chulainn was so embarrassed by being made bald that he went into exile, hiding from his fellow men for a whole year and a day until his hair grew back. He vowed revenge, and so visited Cú Roí's new wife Blathnaid at the fort in Sliabh Mish. She was still very angry at being taken from her home and married against her will, so she was happy to agree to be part of an ambush. She told Cú Chulainn that she would pour milk into the river that ran down alongside the fort, and this would be the signal for him to know that Cú Roí had returned from his travels and for his men to attack.

While celebrating the great festival of Samhain, the knights of the Red Branch were camped on the plain below the fort of Cú Roí. They saw the stream flowing over the edge of the cliff suddenly run white, and they knew that this meant that the king had returned. They scaled the cliffs and broke into the fort, dismembering him where he stood.

Blathnaid tried to escape, but Cú Roí's loyal poet would not let her treachery go unpunished. He ran after her, and, clasping his arms around her body, pushed both of them over the cliffs to their deaths.

THE LEGEND OF MUCKROSS ABBEY

Muckross Abbey, the Franciscan Friary of Irrelagh, was founded by Donal McCarthy Mór in or around 1448. One legend of the abbey's foundation can be found in *History of Ireland* written by Mary Frances Cusack in 1868, although the story is probably much older.

In Cusack's version, the founding site for the friary came to McCarthy Mór in a dream. His dream told him to build the friary at the 'rock of the music'. It is said that he found the spot not far from his home – a rocky area from which beautiful music could mysteriously be heard.

Muckross survived the dissolution of the monasteries by Henry VIII, but in 1589 the monks were expelled from the Abbey by his daughter Elizabeth I. In 1652 it was partially burned by Cromwell's forces during his invasion of Ireland, although the abbey was then reoccupied until 1698. The penal laws meant that the friars faced imprisonment, forcing its closure, with many of them fleeing to France and Spain. Despite the abandonment by the friars it continued to be used as a burial ground, and still is to this day. It is the burial place of local chieftains and the three last great Gaelic poets of the seventeenth and eighteenth centuries – Geoffrey O'Donoghue, Aodhagán O'Rathaille and Eoghan Ruadh Ó Súilleabháin. The abbey, despite missing the main roof, is in great condition and is a popular tourist spot, with the legend of its founding living on in local folklore.

The ruler of thirteenth-century South Munster, Donal McCarthy Mór – also known as King of Desmond – was a leader of great repute. Against a backdrop of conflict with his neighbours (the O'Connors and O'Briens, the Fitzgeralds to the north and the encroaching English) he maintained a proud and independent Gaelic kingdom. He was known for his strength, endurance, intelligence and skill as a clan leader, but also for his ruthlessness and determination.

As he began to move towards old age, he was no longer so concerned with fighting enemies and, as he faced no challenges to his leadership, his kingdom prospered and his territories seemed secure. With his thoughts no longer dominated by concerns of rivalry and struggle, Donal turned to the past and many of the questionable deeds he had done, supposedly for the good of his clan and the kingdom of Desmond. Try as he might to distract himself, his conscience was ill at ease and it troubled him in quiet moments.

After months of being plagued by feelings of doubt and remorse rolled into years, Donal resolved to seek guidance for his troubles. The ageing chieftain sought out a priest and told him of the many things that bothered him. The priest listened carefully to the great McCarthy Mór and then instructed him that he should build an abbey in service of God. Here Donal was to do penance and offer prayers for all of those who had been slaughtered by his hand or at his behest. Donal readily agreed to the priest's words but did not know where he should build it.

'Tell me, holy father, where should I build God's church?'

To which the priest replied in verse:

Signs alone may show,
Thy path of penance eastwards go,
In pilgrim's guise in travel long,
Through summer's heat and winter's snow,
And raise thy fane at rock of song.

Although somewhat bemused by the holy man's rhyme, McCarthy Mór set out on his quest as bidden by the priest. He put aside the garb of a mighty ruler and donned the rough clothes and staff of a pilgrim, setting forth on bare feet in search of the place to build an abbey for the glory of God and the salvation of souls, including his own.

For many months, with just his own thoughts for company, he travelled alone across the countryside; over hills and valleys, through passes and across rivers, hoping to find the place to begin his task. He climbed mountains, asking lonely shepherds if they knew of such a place, and made his way down to the sea where he talked with the fishermen who, like the shepherds, knew nothing of the Rock of Song. After a year and a day spent wandering all over Kerry, Donal became disheartened and began to make his way homeward.

One fine midsummer day on his journey back, he walked along the banks of Lough Lein, where he found a beautiful and sheltered bay set among rocks and woodland. Tired from his long and fruitless travel, McCarthy Mór gathered a bed of ferns to sit down on and rested against the trunk of a great tree. As he sat resting, his mind wandered to his failed quest and he feared that God would not permit him to find the peace that he so yearned for. As dark thoughts descended upon him, he suddenly heard the beautiful sound of a child singing. As Donal listened to the sweet and pure voice ring out in the woods surrounding him, his heart filled with joy and renewed hope. He hoisted his tired body up and began to follow the voice that reminded him of his own boyhood days of purity and innocence, long before pride, power and warring came to dominate his life. As he searched the woods, following the voice, he looked up at a rock near a spring and saw a young girl sat upon it, singing joyfully to herself. At this moment, with tears in his eyes, Donal knew that his search was over – for here before him was the Rock of Song he had looked high and low for.

McCarthy Mór returned to his castle and instructed his men to begin building the abbey on the spot where he had heard the young girl's beautiful singing. He even joined his men, with his own hands, in the construction of the fine abbey and entered the community as a humble friar himself. Here he spent the rest of his days in prayer for the atonement of his own sins and those of others.

TOBAR NA MOLT – WELL OF THE WETHERS

The baptism of Brendan

Not far from Ardfert, in the townland of Tubrid, lies a very famous sacred spring. This spring, which is the source of the Tyshe River, is perhaps the most famous holy well in the county, if not in the entirety of Munster. The name given to this place is Tobar na Molt, or Well of the Wethers, and the reason for this will soon become clear.

It was there that, in the sixth century, a local chieftain by the name of Áirde MacFidaigh took his foster son Mobhí to a holy man for the purpose of baptism. Erc the holy man regularly tended the well, which was broad, clear and deep, and said never to run dry. Many magical and miraculous things are said to reside within its otherworldly waters, and it was frequented by people celebrating both the old religion and the new.

As was common back then, as indeed it still is today, payment was given for the sacrament. For performing the ceremony, Áirde took three rams from his magical flock of purple sheep and gifted them to Erc. These 'fixed' rams, or wethers, were graciously accepted, and this is believed by some to have been the origin of the name of the well.

As the witnesses gathered, Erc proclaimed the event to be a sacred one and put the end of his crozier into the waters of the well, stirring it clockwise three times to awaken it. He then took the child and lay him down by the waters' edge. Placing his healing hands on the boy, he said a quiet prayer before raising his arms skyward to the heavens to prepare himself for the immersion of the child in the waters. Just as he did this, a sudden heavy white mist rolled in and around them. So heavy was it, that the witnesses standing just feet away could see neither Erc nor the child.

Seeing this as a strong sign, Erc took the child and swiftly immersed him in the well – not with the name of Mobhí, but

with the name Bréan Fhionn, meaning white mist. He then
lifted the child out of the water and proclaimed his baptism to
all present before placing him back in his crib to rest. The thick
white mist then dissipated and the three wethers lay against
him, drying the water from his body. His foster mother Ita took
him into her care, and from that day forward the young lad was
no longer referred to as Mobhí, but instead became known as
Bréan Fhionn, or Brendan.

Penal Times

During the dark days of the Penal Times, when the British soldiers were in Ireland, the faithful of the old and new ways usually had a secret hiding place in their locality for to kneel and pray. Tobar na Molt served this purpose, and was one of those rare spaces in the countryside where people could gather and worship in relative safety without fear of assault or death.

All around the slight hollow in which the well sat grew a number of quickset hedges, and it was in these trees that men set up lookout posts with a view in every direction for the priests while they said Mass or carried out their ministries. Should any persons be found gathered at such places, they would be immediately arrested and liable to a flogging by the authorities. The punishment for a priest ministering to the people would be far more severe and it would cost him his life, which is why the people protected their clergy.

One particular pattern day, the people had come as normal to perform the rounds and pay their respects to himself. As is custom, they got down on their knees and prayed at the waters while others tied rags to the nearby bush. It was at this point that one of the lookout men heard the barking of dogs and soon saw the priest-catchers: a group of Redcoats charging across the countryside with their bloodhounds. He gave the nod to the pilgrims and they began to scatter in silence, but as the soldiers were nearly upon them they knew they were done for.

All of a sudden, three purple wethers leapt from the depths of the well and out into the path of the bloodhounds, who, with the smell of fresh meat in their nostrils, changed direction and pursued them in earnest. The Redcoats could do nothing but to abandon their hunt and follow on behind their animals, for they knew that retribution would result from their senior officer for not having control over their dogs. The decoy allowed the priests and the pilgrims to escape.

The hounds pursued the wethers across the land until they reached a flooded ford near the beach at Banna. The wethers jumped into the water and disappeared, not to be seen again. The poor innocent hounds jumped in after them, but were washed out to sea and drowned.

Ever since this time, the place has been known as Áth Caorach or Ford of the Sheep.

THE PHANTOM CITY OF KILSTOHEEN

Across the world there are many and varied stories told of hidden civilisations and forgotten cities, the most well known being that of the famed Atlantis. In fact, Ireland is one of the many lands believed to possess the remains of this metropolis within its offshore waters.

Kerry is no exception to this tradition of magical underwater places, and it is said that an enchanted city known as Kilstoheen, or to give it its proper name, Cill Stuithín, lies beneath the waves of the mighty River Shannon. Between the towns of Ballybunion and Ballylongford, somewhere off the shore of Beale, lies a wondrous place with white quartz buildings, towers and churches, all paved with marble.

Kilstoheen is ruled over by a powerful chieftain called Stuithín, who governs his people with kindness but guards and protects with an iron fist the empire that is named after him. His wizardry allows him to keep a number of charms over the city so that it may be hidden from view at all times, except once every seven years, when it must rise from the depths to allow him to raid the locality for cattle and other livestock to sustain his people. Even at this time, he ensures the protection of his land with a charm that sees any person who witnesses the metropolis surfacing suffer an untimely death within one month – a harsh but necessary measure, in his eyes.

The city is occupied by a mysterious race of beings that possess the power of magic, and use this mostly for their pastime of horse breeding. Their enchanted horses may be seen grazing on moonlit nights in the surrounding fields on the banks of the river, much to the annoyance of local farmers.

In order to remain in their watery paradise, the occupants must not touch earthly soil – if they do, they will become trapped in the earthly realm forever. It is for this reason that they glide just above the ground whenever they leave the city beneath the waves.

There was a farmer by the name of Ned Walsh who lived in a small farmhouse in Cloonaman. Ned's fields sloped right down to the banks of the Shannon and he regularly became fierce annoyed with the strange occurrences that happened in his fields. Every night of the full moon he could hear horses trotting around his pastures while he was in bed. The following mornings he woke to find the fields had been scalped and all manner of vegetation eaten right down to the roots, leaving nothing for his own livestock to feed on.

This happened so often that he vowed to stay up the next night of the full moon, and that was exactly what he did. He watched as nine glowing white stallions trotted right out of the Shannon's waters and up into his field. He gasped in awe as he had never seen such beasts. They walked not on the earth, but glided slightly above it in the air. The horses began ripping clumps of grass out of the ground and swallowing them, then moved on through the hedges, chomping on all the leaves and branches. He became incensed as they ate his field empty. In anger he picked up a sod of turf and, rolling it into a ball, threw it forcefully right at one of the horses. It hit the animal in the side of the belly, and suddenly its glow faded and it glided down to the ground. The other stallions were startled and galloped off down to the shore, right into the waters back to Kilstoheen.

The horse that Ned hit had become an earthly horse and could no longer return to the city as it had touched the soil. He kept it as a workhorse and many people commented on its beauty and strength.

The residents of Kilstoheen still live in their underwater city and, although they keep a decidedly lower profile these days, it is not unknown for the occasional strange thing to happen in the area from time to time around the full moon.

THE BATTLE OF CNOC AN ÁIR

'Cath Chnoic an Áir' is an epic medieval Irish poem of the Fianna (from the Fionn cycle) and was also called 'Laoi Thailc mhic Treoin' (the lay of Tailc mac Treoin). Although it is not one of the most popular myths, it was told in Lady Gregory's *Gods and Fighting Men* and was well known to the people of Kerry into the last century, where the story is thought to have occurred. Here are two stories, the first of which resembles the first part of Gregory's version, while the second story appears to be an amalgam that is only very loosely connected with the final section of Lady Gregory's telling.

While Fionn and the Fianna were camped on the hill of Cnoc an Áir, they passed the time with athletic exercises such as throwing weights and jumping competitions. The Druid of Tara was with their party and he told Fionn that he saw blood in the clouds, an ominous omen. He told Fionn that there was a great deal of trouble soon to descend upon the Fianna. Fionn listened well, but he was not afraid: he was proud of his warriors and he said that the Fianna could stand against any army in the world.

Fionn summoned his grandson Oscar, but Oscar dismissed the omen as unimportant. Fionn sounded the *dordfian*, and with that all of the Fianna came to him. He inspected them all one by one and he found that some of them were afraid, while others were not. Fionn's good friend, Conán mac Morna, was sent to guard a cave and he took some of Aodh Beag's hounds with him. Fionn sounded the *dordfian* again. When Conán heard the sound he ran from the cave. After this, Oscar went to the cave and there he found Aodh Beag guarding it like a warrior.

A beautiful stranger (the daughter of the King of Greece) and her forces came and found the Fianna there. She told them that she had been made to marry Tailc, son of Treon, against her will. He had a face as black as coal and ears and a head like a cat, which is why he was called Tailc King of the Cat Heads. His wife had travelled the world seeking help, but none would give it, until Fionn now offered his protection.

While they were talking, Tailc, who had followed her, appeared with his army. A battalion of a thousand warriors was sent against him but not one returned, and when there was another battalion sent against him they also met their deaths. Oscar asked leave to fight Tailc in single combat and they fought a desperate battle for five days and four nights without food or sleep, until finally Tailc was killed and his head lopped off.

After this, the Fianna raised three loud cheers of sorrow for all their companions who were slain and two of joy for Oscar's victory. When the Fianna came back, they found to their great distress that Tailc's wife was dead. She had died of shame over the great slaughter on her account. Then the Fianna named the hill Cnoc an Áir, which means 'Hill of Slaughter'. The top of the hill is called Leac and it is supposed that those who were killed in the battle were buried there.

A giant came from Limerick to Leathárdán in North Kerry. He came to a house and asked the woman of the house what were the men doing, and she told him that they were minding bulls on the hill nearby. He asked her what feats the men performed and she told him of their throwing a stone that was 7 tons over the castle. The giant said he would try it and he threw the stone over the castle easily and caught it at the other side again, which amazed the woman.

The giant asked her to serve him dinner, so she gave him a 'piggon' of milk and a cake of bread with a griddle in between it because she wanted to know if he had strong teeth. He broke the griddle and threw it aside and ate up the bread and drank the milk. He asked her if it was the same food the child in the cradle was getting and she said it was. He asked her if the baby had teeth and she asked him to put his fingers in the baby's mouth but he did not.

Then the men of the house came home – namely Fionn, Oscar, Conán-Maol, Oisín, Cúchulainn, Murchadha and Hear-Well. They sent the giant to a glen to get a bull, knowing full well that anyone that ever went into the glen was killed by it. The giant killed the bull and brought him home and roasted him and they all had a fine dinner of it. When they were eating the bull, Oscar and the Limerick giant halved a hock of beef and ate a half each.

The giant decided it was time to return home to Limerick and on his way he went to the hill of Knockanore (Cnoc an Áir) and met Conán-Maol. The giant said that he should get a bull to take home. The two of them killed the bull by catching a horn each and they split him in half, but they did not take the bull home. After a time, the giant invited the seven Fianna men to his castle but only three of them went with him.

When they arrived at the castle, there was a big table of beef ready for them and there were many chairs around the table. When they had eaten, the men of the Fianna found that they were stuck to the chairs and the chairs were themselves stuck to the floor. The giant went to another castle to collect his men to kill his guests and in due course they killed the Fianna. Oscar, however, was not fully dead. The giant's men had lost their legs or feet in the conflict, but were still alive and so the giant's wife brought a bottle of magical potion to cure them. When she was crossing by Oscar, he tripped her up and some of the liquid in the bottle fell on him and the instant he was healed he jumped up and killed her.

He took up the bottle and rubbed the potion on his own companions and they were all as good as ever. Once recovered they killed the Limerick men and then they took the castle, but Fionn was stuck to a glass door and he could not pull himself away. Oscar, being the strongest man, caught him by the hands and gave him a pull and left all his back skin stuck to the glass. Conán-Maol went and got a sheep and skinned it and put it red hot up to Fionn's back and so he was alright again. The sheep skin continued to grow wool, enough to clothe seven men.

THE ORIGIN OF THE KILLARNEY LAKES

Long ago, in Ireland's ancient past – before the Milesians, Tuatha Dé Danann or even the Firbolgs had set foot upon the shores of Ireland – the area of land now occupied by the three lakes of Killarney was a stretch of green and pleasant valley, wherein a peaceful and happy people once lived.

The land was flourishing, with an abundance of fruit trees in the multitude of orchards, fine seasonal crops from rolling fields that had the very best of soil, healthy game in great numbers in the forest around, and plenty of fish from the rivers and streams that flowed through the area. No people could say that they were more blessed by the gifts of nature than the ancient denizens of this happy valley, and indeed the people were both healthy and merry.

The only minor regret the residents might have was that there were not more springs to drink from and that there was but one well in the place to serve the needs of the people. This well was of great value to the people of the valley and they placed great importance on its maintenance and care. A law was passed for its protection that, when not in use for drawing water, the well should be covered over with a lid at all times. Over the years this rule had always been observed and it became a tradition that, should the well be left uncovered, a great disaster would befall the area and its people.

The chieftain of this ancient people was a just and wise ruler who lived simply and frugally in the same manner as the rest of his people. The chieftain lived alone save for his only child – his daughter Eileen who had grown into a tall and beautiful young woman. One fine summer afternoon Eileen made her way down to the well with a large pitcher, as she was often prone to do, to bring back fresh water to the house.

She took a refreshing drink herself before filling up the pitcher from the well and as she readied herself to return home, a handsome young stranger approached. The young man, who she had never seen before, bowed to her and politely asked to slake his thirst after his long journey. Eileen of course offered him some water and the two sat down to talk a while. The young man was a warrior and he told her of his exploits in a war far away from the pleasant valley, and she was utterly enthralled by his tale.

With his eloquence and charm, the warrior made a deep impact upon the young lady and, as the sun slowly sank into the west, Eileen began to fall madly in love with him. As the darkness grew, she was saddened by the thought of parting so soon after they had met, so she asked the young warrior to accompany her home to meet her father. He too was deeply smitten by the beautiful young woman and readily agreed, carrying the pitcher for her as they strolled back towards the chief's house.

In her newfound joy at their unexpected meeting, Eileen did what no one had done previously: she forgot to replace the cover of the beloved well-spring.

That night, as the people of the valley slept soundly and peacefully, the great calamity they all feared began to take place. The spring that fed the well grew as the night passed, until the well filled up and eventually overflowed. At first it was no more than a trickle that splashed down upon the ground, but it steadily increased and in no time at all it became a huge torrent that flowed across the valley. Hour by hour the waters rose, filling every hollow and surging across the land as the people continued to sleep, blissfully unaware of the danger. It was not until the waters rose to meet the houses that the first of the people awoke as their homes became flooded with the ever-increasing flow of water.

In their fear and confusion in the darkness no one could see where the water was coming from, but before long they guessed that their well had been left uncovered, although by now it was far too late to remedy the situation.

In desperation, some brave souls swam out to the well and dived down in hope of replacing the cover to save their beloved valley from disaster. All those who did so were lost to the rising waters and were not seen again.

Realising that it was hopeless to continue, the people of the valley resolved to abandon their homes and escape. Some clutching a few possessions and most just running as fast as they could, the villagers tried to make it to the higher ground of the surrounding mountain slopes. Sadly, not even the young people were fast enough to outrun the waters that swelled and boiled ferociously with ever-increasing vigour. Even the great chieftan, his daughter Eileen and her companion were swept away by the raging waters and, like the rest of the people, they were drowned.

By the time the sun rose again over the beautiful valley, there was no more valley to be seen. Every homestead, tree, field, beast and person was submerged under the waters of the three lakes that had sprung up overnight.

Silence descended over the now calm waters of the Killarney Lakes, but this was not entirely the end of the story. It is said that the people of the valley were carried by the raging waters to Tír na n-Óg and their spirits returned to their home underneath the lake. On certain calm and misty nights, at certain times of year, the ancient spirits of the valley can be glimpsed upon the waters of the lakes.

Even now, the jarvies (hackney coach or jaunting car drivers) and the boatmen of the lakes might tell you, if anyone should be so bold as to dive to the bottom of the largest lake and replace the cover that still lies there, then the waters of the lake would gradually subside to reveal again the once splendid valley. The tragic forgetfulness of that ancient chieftain's daughter was the making of one of Kerry's most famed places of beauty, renowned throughout Ireland and beyond. No one has tried to replace the cover, as far as can be told, for who would want to see an end to the great beauty of the lakes of Killarney?

CASTLEISLAND CASTLE

Castleisland Castle, also referred to as 'the Castle on the Island' or simply 'the Island', was once the centre of Desmond power in County Kerry, and gave its name to the small town that surrounds the one remaining tower of the once proud castle. The castle was built in 1226 by Geoffrey de Marisco, Lord Justice of Ireland, during the reign of Henry III of England. His daughter Eleanor married Thomas Fitzmaurice, thereby bringing the castle into the possession of the Desmond family.

Maurice Fitzgerald, the 1st Earl of Desmond, rebelled against the English Crown in 1345. In that same year, the castle was attacked by Sir Ralph Ufford, who was hoping to capture the earl. The castle was being held for the earl by three knights – Sir Eustace de la Poer, John Coterel and William Grant. When it was captured by Ufford (Lord Justice of Ireland), the three of them were hanged, drawn and quartered. Despite losing the castle and all his lands, and being imprisoned in London, Maurice managed to convince the Crown of his loyalty and was pardoned in 1349, even becoming Lord Justice of Ireland in 1355, shortlyly before his death.

His descendants continued to hold the castle. The 3rd Earl, Gerald, was a man of great learning and a fine poet, but he was also reputed to have been a magician and involved in black magic. He disappeared from the castle in 1398, presumably murdered. The 6th Earl, James Fitzgerald – who had gained his earldom by deposing his nephew for marrying into a Gaelic family – signed a peace treaty at the castle in 1422.

During the conflict with the rival Ormond family, Gerald Fitzgerald, the 15th Earl, was imprisoned in the Tower of London, but returned to Castleisland in 1565. After a second imprisonment, Gerald returned to Castleisland in 1573 and rebelled until his death in 1583. He and his wife narrowly escaped capture at the castle in 1580, when attacked by Sir William Pelham. Following the last Earl's death, the castle and all the surrounding Desmond lands were given to Sir William Herbert of Wales in 1583. He restored the castle in 1586, but in 1661 Thomas Herbert made plans to move the family to a new mansion. In 1686 the new house was finally completed nearby and the Herberts let the castle fall into ruin. Parts of the castle were used to build in the nearby town, leading it to becoming the small remains that exist now. The following stories about the castle were gathered in the 1930s.

We have in this town the ruins of a very old castle. The ruins are now seven hundred years old. Our house is built from the stones of this castle. One of our neighbours when digging in her garden unearthed some bloodstained stones and a part of an altar, which was bought by an American. There are many secret passages in the castle. At the centre of the castle there is a big hole and inside this hole there is a large flagstone. Underneath this flagstone there is a path which leads into the road. In the olden times the soldiers used to go through this passage in order to escape the enemy. One day my grandmother told me that she climbed the castle and when she was nearly at the top of it she saw a quaint little room. She forced her way into it and as soon as she entered a stone moved on the wall. She went over to it and found a small box with something rusty inside in it.

There are many stories told about the old castle in Castleisland and many of those were handed down from generation to generation. One of the most commonly told tales concerning the castle is that after the death of Sir Maurice Fitzgerald his sister inherited the castle. She is said to have married a wizard who was noted for his magic powers. She often begged him to demonstrate his magic arts for her but he always refused.

One day, after long pleading on her part, he finally promised to grant her wish on the condition that she would show no sign of fear, regardless of what happened. She was delighted and readily agreed to his terms. Just as it does now, the River Maine flowed beneath the castle walls. The magician leapt out of the window into the river below and much to the delight of his curious wife, changed himself

into many different creatures. After many changes, he took the form
of a huge and terrible monster and opening his wide and fearful
jaws, made his way towards her. Despite her promise to show no
fear, this proved too much for her and she yelled and screamed for
protection. Her screams and shouts had the tragic effect of break-
ing the spell and the unfortunate man was unable to resume his
human shape.

The poor magician, unable to become human again, turned
into a goose and flew to a lake near Limerick where it is said he
remained until his death. The poor unhappy wife, the cause of all
the misfortune, regretted her thoughtlessness and in her distress sent
many messages to her lord begging him to return. Sadly the magi-
cian was powerless to undo the effects of the magic and so spent the
rest of his days in banishment and solitude.

THE HIDDEN TREASURE OF KNOCKANE

There are many stories of hidden treasure in County Kerry,
several of which focus on Knockane. As it happens, there is
more than one place called Knockane – one near Listowel, one
near Tralee, and one near Annascaul – and, according to some
accounts, the place is also often confused with Knockanore in
County Waterford, which reputedly also held a hidden treasure.

Here we have some intriguing stories of Knockane and its
treasure, collected in the 1930s by children. They may not be
entirely accurate but as the saying goes: why let the truth spoil
a good story?

Long ago, some people buried their gold under a sceach bush
(whitethorn / hawthorn).

There is a place in Dirha, not far from Listowel, and this
place is the Knockane we are concerned with. Here a large and
impressive sceach grew, and hearing of the treasure that lay

buried beneath, a local man went digging. He dug down and came upon a flagstone, but suddenly a big bull came up and chased him away from the hole.

The man came back the next day, but once again the bull chased him away. Once again he returned, but this time he came prepared with a bottle of holy water in his pocket. The bull arrived once more, snorting and stamping his hooves, but when the man shook the holy water over the bull it ran away.

The man continued his digging undisturbed and finally he found a pot of gold.

Long ago, people believed that there were pots of gold under a hill of gravel called Knockane, which was in the bog at Dirha, near Listowel. One night, two men went out to dig up the gold that was believed to be buried there. No sooner had they started digging than a band of fairies appear in front of them, and so the two men ran for their lives and that was enough for them so far as treasure was concerned. The next morning two men were in a woeful state, as one fella's hair had turned white with fear, while the other's mouth was stretched wide almost to his ears.

One night a man was out walking and he heard a voice that said to him 'dig, dig, dig', but chose to ignore it. The next night he walked the same way and heard the voice once more, telling him the same thing. On the third night the man walked that way again, hearing the voice once more. He decided to dig at the very spot and after some hard work he found the most bizarre thing: a horse's skin which contained a bucket full of dead insects. He left the bucket where he found it but told his friends the whole story. On the fourth night he returned but this time with his friends and a bottle of holy water. He sprinkled the holy water on the insects and to their amazement the insects were transformed into gold coins.

Michael Connor of Dirha dreamt the same dream three nights in succession. He dreamt that there was a pot of gold buried in the Knockane in Dirha, Listowel. He asked his friends Thomas Connor and Paddy O'Driscoll to go with him and dig it up. At about eleven o'clock that night they began, bringing, of all things, a cock with them. When they arrived at the Knockane they put the cock in a tree and began to dig, but they found nothing worth mentioning. The cock began to crow at which Thomas Connor and Paddy Driscoll ran away in fear and Michael Connor began to yell as he had become stuck in the hole. Michael's friends gathered their senses and went back for him, pulled him out of the hole and the cock too. They all made it back home safely, but the next morning when the arose they found that the cock was dead.

There is a fort in Knockane near Clounmacon, Listowel, in which there are stone steps leading down to an underground passage. In the past it was said that a man living close by had gone down the steps and searched for hidden treasure. After much digging and exploration, he came to a flagstone under which he discovered a pot of gold.

The Legend of Torc Waterfall

Many moons ago, in a time when people were still wary of fairies, pookas and such like, there lived a good man by the name of Larry Hayes in Clohereen, where he worked his small farm in poverty. Larry was as honest and decent a man as anyone could hope to meet, and he worked hard too, but despite this he never seemed to have any luck.

His few cattle, sheep and horses had a nasty habit of falling into trouble if he was ever to leave them out for a night. They would either be found lame the next day, go missing or, if he was really unlucky, turn up stone dead the next morning. Larry wracked his brain as to the cause of his terrible bad luck, but he could think of nothing. He had always tried to do the right thing and he could think of no one who disliked him, or who he'd made an enemy of that might curse him, or otherwise try to harm him.

After days and weeks ran into months, Larry's luck still didn't change and he remained mystified. He resolved to try and solve the mysterious happenings once and for all by staying up all night on his farm, even though he was somewhat fearful of the 'Good People', like many others. So one night, close to midnight, Larry left the comfort of his family and fire in the little cottage they had, and set out into his fields to keep watch on the farm. After some considerable time spent wandering up and down, nothing of note had happened and he was becoming quite bored of his lonely vigil.

Just at the point when Larry had decided he'd had enough and turned to go back to the cottage, he saw a huge boar appear in front of him. It was so sudden and unexpected that Larry almost died of fright right there on the spot, but as the boar remained calm and still he soon recovered his composure and blessed himself.

'What in the name of God are you?' he uttered quietly, more to himself than to the beast. To his great surprise, the boar answered him in a human voice.

'I am under an enchantment.'

The poor farmer stood frozen in disbelief, just starring at the boar, who continued to speak.

'I'm very sorry, but it was I who killed your animals, after all I am transformed into a wild boar. I'd like to make it up to you though as I can see you are poor. Come with me and I can make you richer than you can imagine and I promise no harm shall come to you.' The boar seemed genuine enough to Larry and although he was still somewhat fearful he decided to follow the boar, who led him into the nearby Torc Woods.

After a short while they arrived at a cliff face of solid rock, in which a door mysteriously appeared. The boar pushed the door open and instantly transformed back into the form of a young man as he entered the chamber beyond. Following inside, Larry was amazed by the sumptuous interior of the room, which was lavishly decorated. He was even more amazed to be invited to dine on a grand feast of beef, mutton and fine drink that appeared on the large table in front of them. After they had dined, the young man excused himself briefly and returned with a small bag that he laid on the table in front of Larry.

Larry was both astonished and delighted to find that it was a bag of gold coins.

'There's plenty more of that, should you need it,' said the young man. 'As long as you promise not to tell a living soul of what you have seen tonight. If you can keep this secret between us for seven years, then you'll be a rich man for the rest of your life. If you fail, then it will be the ruin of both of us.'

Larry swore that he would tell no one of the young man, his enchantment as a boar, or of his hidden home. Giving his thanks, he left the rock and made his way home with the bag of gold coins.

After a short time, Larry's wife began to notice his sudden change in circumstances and wondered where all this money had come from. No doubt their neighbours were equally curious about the miraculous change of fortune. However, no matter how he was quizzed and cajoled, he would not reveal the source of his newfound wealth. Eventually friends and neighbours grew tired of asking him to no avail, but Larry's wife would not give up so easily. Driven to distraction with frustration, she secretly followed him on one of the rare occasions when he returned to the rock one night.

To her surprise, she saw the door open in the rock face and her husband disappearing inside. After waiting a while, he re-emerged clutching a small bag of coins and, as he made to return home, she confronted him in a state of anger and distress.

'How can you keep such a secret from your own wife, the mother of your dear children?'

After much berating from his wife, Larry finally gave in and told her what had happened to change his terrible luck.

No sooner had he done so, than the boar appeared on the top of the rock face and bellowed out in great anger. 'You fool, you have finished us both!'

As the bewildered couple looked on, the mountain rocked like an earthquake. The boar was suddenly swept up into the air in a ball of fire, before he was carried off to Poul an Ifrinn and plunged into the waters of the Punch Bowl lake. No sooner had this happened, than the earth and rocks moved and a great cascade of water began to poor down the hillside and over the rock face. In terror, Larry and his wife scrambled out of the way of the descending water, leaving behind the gold he had been given in their desperate climb. The waters crashed down, concealing forever the rock face and creating the mighty Torc Waterfall. Badly shaken, the couple staggered back to their farm but, as the enchanted young man had predicted, Larry's good fortune deserted him. Very soon, he was poorer than he had ever been and was forced to wander the land as a vagrant for the rest of his days.

5

MYTHICAL CREATURES

HIS MAJESTY KING PUCK

If you ever visit the fine town of Killorglin, you may notice that on the banks of the River Laune there is a rather conspicuous statue. A fine bronze sculpture by Alan Ryan Hall, which is in the form of a proud puck goat standing aloft a large rock. If you look even closer, you will see that the puck is wearing something unusual on his head – a crown.

Sometime in the 1600s, the bold Oliver Cromwell and his Roundheads were up to their old tricks of sacking villages and kidnapping locals in Kerry. While on their way to cause havoc in Killorglin, they passed through the hilly area around Kilgobnet and spotted a herd of wild mountain goats grazing on the lower slopes of the MacGillycuddy's Reeks. For some perverse entertainment, they decided to charge the poor animals with their bayonets brandished, and this caused them to scatter in fear of their lives.

The herd turned sharply and ran uphill to the safety of the cliffs, ledges and crags of the mountain, while one particular puck goat broke away from the herd and ran downhill towards

the town. As the brave animal reached the environs of the town it collapsed in exhaustion and the townspeople immediately ran to its aid. They knew by this unusual sight alone that there was something not quite right, and so they ordered all the children indoors and locked up all the livestock before barricading themselves inside the town.

The Roundheads finally reached the town some hours later and tried to push their way inside. Having little success, they fired a number of volleys into the town in a further act of provocation, but could get neither access nor reaction. They finally gave up and departed, much to the Killorglin people's delight and relief, and they vowed to celebrate their saviour with the highest honour possible, the kingship.

Every year in August, a three-day festival is held in honour of the goat that saved Killorglin from the ravages of Cromwell.

A wild mountain puck goat is taken from the uplands and crowned as King Puck for the festival, and the celebrations go on late into each night.

It is said that during the festival, puck looks down and acts the king while people look up and act the goat!

THE DULLAHAN

While it will be of no surprise to many to hear of the vast array of fairy beings in Ireland, not many will have heard of the Dullahan, even though it will greet us all at least once in our lifetimes. The appearance of the spirit is said to be of a tall, dark humanoid, dressed in long flowing robes and sitting on a carriage pulled by two shiny black stallions with glowing red eyes. The horses are spurred onwards by constant strikes administered by the Dullahan with a whip made from a human spine. Of course, if this were not terrifying enough, the most frightening visual of the beast is that it is completely headless, carrying its severed head in its arms as it gallops across the countryside.

Elena Danaan

The Dullahan is believed to be the incarnation of Crom Dubh, the pagan god who needed human sacrifices to sustain its existence during the time of the old religions. When the masses turned away from paganism, it found itself morphing into death's herald in its current form, enabling it to continue seizing souls.

The Dullahan has fantastic eyesight, even on the darkest of nights, and in order to see where it is going it holds its head high in the air.

Whenever the creature is seen or heard coming, it is wise to run, hide and cover your ears – for if it passes you on the road it may throw a crock of blood in your face, or strike you blind as it goes. Alternatively, if it is your soul it seeks, it may call your name and leave you with an uncontrollable urge to climb into its carriage, allowing it to take you to the underworld.

The Dullahan is particularly prevalent around midnight on the old Irish feasts, particularly on Samhain or Hallowe'en, and sudden fires along the roadsides on winter nights may be a sign of its recent visit to the area.

There is but one defence against the Dullahan, as described in the story below.

It was one particular Hallowe'en night in the county, on the outskirts of the village of Ballyheigue to be specific, when the Clifford family were safe at home playing some games, as is traditional on this night. All of a sudden, they heard the hooves of horses outside their window, followed by violent snorts, the likes of which they had never heard before.

Mr Clifford poked out from behind the curtains of their little cottage, only to be greeted by the bulging red eye of one of the Dullahan's horses. In terror, he shouted to his family to cover their ears. He looked out once more only to see the beast pointing its bony finger at him through the pane of glass – only then did he realise that his time had come. Seeing what was happening, Mrs Clifford ran to her nightstand and pulled out an old gold tooth which belonged to her grandfather. Before her husband's name could be uttered, she flung the tooth at the window, and with a large shriek, the laneway outside the cottage was quickly silent once more.

'What have you done, woman?' asked Mr Clifford with a tremble in his voice.

'Sure, isn't the only thing that the Dullahan is afraid of is gold?' Mrs Clifford said. The poor man broke down in tears.

'Isn't it only my life you have saved on this night!' he said and gathered his family together in thanksgiving of the second chance he had been given.

PORT NA BPÚCAÍ

It was an unusually warm spring evening on An Blascaod Mór. The sea was as calm as a purring cat and as flat as a sheet of glass. A mild breeze caressed the soft mossy blanket that covered the island, and anybody who had the opportunity was fast asleep in the little huts and cabins that hugged the sloping hills all around the island.

A few of the islanders were still awake, however, as the call of duty on this remote place never ceased. Two fishermen silently rowed back in their currach towards the harbour. A woman wrapped in her long shawl lingered on Trá Bhán, gathering mussels at low tide. An old fiddler, having a sneaky nightcap while his wife was out, played one last tune on the stool outside his home.

It was these that heard it.

All of a sudden, from the unseen depths of the ocean, the echo of a haunting melody rose and rode the waves. It travelled on the breeze and curled around the hills, speaking to the trees and whispering at the windows.

The men in the currach laid down their oars and listened intently to the lament that permeated the skin of their wee boat, not quite believing what they were hearing. The woman hoisted up her large skirt over her knees and ran back to her cottage to find her husband. She thought he would be fast asleep, but found him outside sitting on a stool and mesmerised by what was coming in on the breeze.

She knelt down at his feet and he put his arm around her while they both looked out over the water and listened, with tears in their eyes, to the air that came straight from the spirits of the sea.

Elena Danaan

All who heard it were frozen in time at the beauty of what they were experiencing, and they remained so until the first ray of the morning sun shone the next day.

The fiddler knew that he had a duty to record what they had heard and so 'Port na bPúcaí' or 'Lament of the Fairies' was reproduced, and thanks to him it still exists to this day.

THE ENCHANTED HARE

There was a strong farmer one time and he had nine beautiful cows, all grazing on the best of land. Surely that was a great prosperity, and you'd be thinking him the richest man in all of Kerry. But it was little milk he was getting from his nine lovely cows, and no butter from the milk.

They'd be churning in that house for three hours or maybe for five hours of a morning, and at the end of it all a few wee grains of butter is all they'd be rewarded with – the size of which would be no bigger than robin's eggs floating on the top of the milk. Even that much did not remain to it, for when herself ran the strainer in under them they melted from the churn.

There were great confabulations held about the loss of the yield, but the strength of the spoken word was powerless to restore what was gone. Herself began to think that himself had been struck down with the evil eye, and it was overlooking his own cattle he was by walking through them and he fasting at the dawn of day.

The notion didn't please him too well; indeed, he was horrid vexed at her for saying the like, but he went no more among the cows until after his breakfast time. Sure that did no good at all – it was less and less milk that was coming in each day. And butter going a lovely price in the market, to leave it a worse annoyance to have none for to sell.

The man of the house went out walking with his dog that evening and, to their utter shock, they saw a hare running with the nine cows through the field. The hound took off after the hare and followed it through the quicken hedge, over the ditches, and down past the lake.

Himself remembered a story his father once told him about hares being enchanted people. He said to himself, 'I don't know if is true or not, but there's something not quite right about about these things at all.'

There was a small, wee house up an old boreen, and that was where the hunt headed for. The hare ran up the lane not a yard in front of the hound, and made a leap for to get into the cabin by a wee hole in the wall. The hound got a grip of it, and took a chunk out of its side before the hare disappeared into the hole.

They pulled open the door and ran inside the old derelict shack, looking around for the injured hare. They heard some rustling in the next room, and with that pushed into the kitchen. There was neither sight nor sign of a hare to be found, but an old woman lay in a corner and she was bleeding.

The dog gave out an awful whine and pushed his nose into his master's feet, given the odious dread it felt.

The farmer then turned and left for home, saying, 'Surely there's not a many in the world do be hunting hares through the fields and catching old women bleeding to death.'

On reaching his front gate, herself came running out shouting with glee: 'Will you look at the gallons of beautiful milk the cows are after giving this day!' And sure enough, from that day to this, there was a great plenty of milk and a right yield of butter on the churn.

6

QUARE HAPPENINGS AND CAUTIONARY TALES

GHOST OF THE *DRONNINGEN*

A Norweigan ship by the name of *Dronningen* was wrecked in a violent storm off the coast of Leck Point, Ballybunion, in the year 1882. With a crew of eighteen men and one faithful dog, it had left Norway and called at Glasgow to pick up an 11,000 tonne cargo of coal to deliver to America, where it would then collect a cargo of wheat for transport back. As it left the safety of the Scottish harbour, a sudden storm whipped up and the ship and its poor crew were tossed in all directions. The captain decided that the storm would not last and so pressed on with the voyage.

The captain and crew sailed south from Glasgow and down past the Isle of Man into the Celtic Sea, where they hugged the coast until they got to the region of Ballybunion. It was from there that they hoped to take a straight westerly course directly to America, but the storm was relentless and the waves unforgiving. The ferocious wind and rain picked up even more, and suddenly the boat lost its rudder. This was as good as a death sentence for any ship in a storm, but the men persevered as hardened sailors do. The wind and waves gradually began to push the ship in towards the coast and onto the rocks towards Lick Castle.

Their trusty dog seized the opportunity and, taking a rope in his mouth, jumped overboard and swam towards Leck Point, where some locals were watching to see if they could be of any help. When the dog came ashore, the men took the rope and tied it around a number of large trees as an anchor. The sailors were then able to scoot along the rope from the stricken vessel to the safety of land. The faithful dog ran back along the rope and onto the ship to see if anybody else was left behind, but just as he did the ship was swamped by a rogue wave and the poor dog drowned.

The grateful men were given comfort in Ballybunion for a few days while they recovered from their ordeal. Word was sent back to Norway of the happening and a recovery ship was sent to collect the crew from Limerick.

The wreck of the *Dronningen* was slowly taken by the tide, but at certain parts of the year when the water is unusually low, rusted parts of the ship can still be seen wedged in among the rocks at Leck.

Some also say that on certain nights, around the anniversary of when the ship was wrecked, a bright light can be seen far out to sea off Leck Point, and one would be forgiven for assuming that it is a flare lit by far-off fishermen. The light would gradually draw in closer and closer to the shore, and land on the rocky point where the ship was wrecked. It would then take the form of the ghostly apparition of a dog running along the rocks with a rope in its mouth, until it finally disappears. Few have seen this spectre, but those that have all say that it is the ghost of the poor dog that saved the crew that day and paid the price with his life. Another unfortunate aspect to this tale is that the dog's name is not remembered, even to this day.

DARBY RED BEARD'S CASTLE IN THE LAND OF NOWHERE

A long time ago there lived a king in Castle Farm, and he had one son who was the best handball player in all of Ireland. The king built a large alley for his son in the castle yard as a place where he could practice.

One morning the son went out to play handball and he unexpectedly met a little man waiting for him. The little man challenged the boy to play a game and the king's son agreed, and they played for the granting of any request.

To the son's surprise, he was sorely beaten by the little man and so had to fulfill his request. The little man tasked the king's son with finding Darby Red Beard's castle in the Land of Nowhere, and bringing back home with him the cloak of darkness, the sword of lightning, and the seven league boots.

The little man gave him a year and a day to do the job, but no clue as to how to complete his task. The king's son told his father of the match with the odd little man and the bizarre task assigned to him. The king didn't know of this place, but gave his son a magic ball and told him follow the ball wherever it would go.

And so the boy started out on his journey and the ball led him to a castle in a lonely wood. The boy knocked at the door and asked lodgings for the night and was made welcome by an old man who owned the castle. When asked about his business, the king's son told the old man how he had come to be there. The old man listened carefully, then told him go to visit his brother, who was 100 years older than himself and lived in a castle not far away. The brother, he said, would be able to offer more help than he.

The following morning the king's son set out and, after a few hours, arrived at the brother's castle. The owner was a very wizened old man and he welcomed the king's son.

'Well young fella,' he said, 'I know where you are headed and you have a hard job alright. I am six hundred years old and I have never heard tell of the Land of Nowhere. Don't lose heart though, as I have command over the birds of the air and perhaps they can be of assistance.'

The next morning, when the son was ready to leave, the old man blew his whistle and a multitude of birds came to him. To the son's surprise the old man could converse with the birds, and he asked them if they had ever heard of the Land of Nowhere. Not one of them knew of it, but they said there was one bird missing, the giant eagle of Blue Mountain, who might know it.

And so the old man blew his whistle again, but the eagle did not come. After a few more blows on the whistle, the eagle finally appeared in the distance and flew in to land at his feet.

'Where were you when I first blew my whistle?' the old man asked him.

'I was feeding my young ones,' the bird replied.

'Where were you when I blew the second time?' asked the old man.

The eagle replied, 'I was passing Darby Red Beard's Castle in the Land of Nowhere.'

'Very good,' he said. 'I was hoping you might know of this place. Will you please take this boy to Darby Red Beard's Castle?'

'All right,' the bird replied, 'but I must have food first.' So the old man killed a fat bullock, and the eagle ate his fill.

After the eagle had eaten, the king's son got on his back and away the bird flew, over many mountains, lakes and valleys, until he landed at Darby Red Beard's Castle. The boy got off the eagle's back and made his way into the castle, where he asked Darby Red Beard for the cloak of darkness, the sword of lightning, and the seven league boots. To the boy's surprise, Darby Red Beard immediately agreed to give them, but then added the condition that the boy complete three tasks for him the next day.

The first task was to drain the water from a lake and find a ring that was at the bottom. The second task was to clean out a stable that had not been cleaned for 100 years, and find a needle that was lost there. The third and final task was to build a house and thatch the roof with one feather from every bird in the air. The king's son's heart sank as he pondered how he could complete three seemingly impossible tasks. Nonetheless, the boy started his first task early the next morning by bailing the lake with a bucket. As fast as he bailed the water out, the lake filled up again: it was hopeless. The poor lad did not know what to do and he sat down on the shore until a young girl arrived carrying his breakfast. She asked him what he was doing there and he explained to her that he had to drain the lake, but he had given up. She told him not to be troubled, and said that she would help him. The girl took up the bucket, threw out just one scoop of water and the lake miraculously dried up. She walked out into the dried-up lake and shortly returned with the ring, handing it to the dumbstruck boy, who was delighted.

'I have still another task to do,' said the king's son. 'I have to clean out a filthy stable.'

The girl smiled. 'I will do it for you,' she said. When they reached the stable she threw out just one shovelful, after which all the manure disappeared instantly to reveal the needle, which she handed to the boy.

'I still have one last task left,' he said. 'I must build a house and thatch it with feathers from all the birds of the air.'

Once more the girl offered to help. 'I will do it for you,' she said. The girl whistled gently, summoning the birds of the air and – to the lad's amazement – she had it built and thatched well in time for dinner.

The king's son went back to Darby Red Beard and told him that the three tasks were completed. He handed over the ring and needle, and pointed out the little house from a castle window.

'I have done my part,' he said. 'Now, please may I have the cloak of darkness, the sword of lightning, and the seven league boots, as promised?'

The Darby duly handed them over. The king's son was so delighted with his secret helper, that he brought her on the long journey home to his father's castle. The king was overjoyed to welcome home his son, and the boy presented the three treasures to the little old man, who smiled and disappeared, never to be heard from again.

The king's son asked the girl who had helped him in his adventures to be his wife, and the two of them lived happily until the end of their days.

A Strange Tale of Oliver Cromwell

As a young boy Timothy Lawlor, from Ballyduff wrote down a strange tale of Oliver Cromwell he'd heard, which is retold here.

Oliver Cromwell is perhaps the most reviled person in the whole of Irish history and this story, which is completely factually incorrect, says more about wishful thinking than it does about Cromwell himself.

Oliver Cromwell was merely a cobbler's son before joining the British Army and he gave up his religion and came to Ireland. One day he was going through Limerick and he happened upon a saint who was fishing. Cromwell took the net from the saint and he threw it out into the river and caught a trout. He cut the tail off of the trout and threw it into the river again and caught it once more. He asked the saint if he had ever seen anyone do that and the saint replied that no one could do that except Oliver Cromwell.

Cromwell wrote a letter and he gave it to the saint, asking him to deliver it to an officer in Cork. What did the saint do, but gave it to Cromwell's brother, and the brother then delivered the letter to the officer. The officer read the letter, and the instructions that were in it were to shoot the bearer, and so the officer shot Cromwell's brother, because he had delivered the letter. Oliver Cromwell thought that the saint would deliver the letter, but the saint was too clever for him.

Cromwell asked the saint before he sent him to Cork how long would he reign in Ireland, and the saint said that if Cromwell crossed a certain bridge in Limerick he would live for a very long time. When Cromwell was about a quarter of a mile from the bridge his horse lost one of its shoes and so Cromwell took his horse back to a nearby forge to get a shoe fitted. The blacksmith had no iron to make a new shoe, but he did have an old musket and he put it in the fire to melt it and blew the bellows. The musket, which was loaded, went off, shooting Cromwell dead where he stood and so he never crossed the bridge alive.

Oliver Cromwell was actually born into minor English gentry, not as described above – and he certainly would not have given up his religion, which led him to commit terrible crimes against Catholics, in Ireland in particular.

Cromwell was one of ten children, but none of his brothers survived their childhood, highlighting another inaccuracy of this story, which describes Cromwell's betrayal backfiring on him.

Cromwell didn't die in Ireland and was probably never in Limerick. The Siege of Limerick took place some months after he returned to England in 1650, and at the time of the siege he was leading the war against Scotland, where Charles II had been proclaimed king. Most Irish people would have been delighted had he died while in Ireland, but Cromwell in fact died in 1658; not by gunshot, but from an unglamorous infection that was probably caused by severe kidney stones.

Interestingly, Cromwell was hated almost as much in England and Scotland as he was in Ireland, and in 1661 his body was dug up on the twelfth anniversary of Charles I's execution. His corpse was tried, found guilty of regicide, bound in chains and hanged. After his posthumous execution, he was beheaded and the body was dismembered and thrown into a pit. Cromwell's head was displayed on a pole for nearly twenty-five years outside Westminster Hall in London, until 1685, when it blew down in a storm.

Found by an unknown passer-by, the head remained unrecovered for years until it was sold to Swiss collector, Claudius De Puy. The head changed hands many times over the centuries, even losing an ear due to mistreatment along the way. After appearing in a museum for some time the head was privately bought and studied to prove its authenticity. Finally, in 1960, some 300 years after his death, Cromwell's head was buried in the Antechapel of Sidney Sussex College, Cambridge, but his body has never been recovered. The true story of Oliver Cromwell's end is probably a more fitting and ignoble one than his demise in this rather confused child's story.

How Loughfouder got its Name

Long, long ago, there lived in Loughfouder a very famous man by the name of Brooder or, in Irish, Bruadar. This man was reputed to be very rich indeed and it was for this reason that he attracted the attention of some robbers.

Bruadar was accustomed to going rambling to visit his neighbours by night, and the robbers became aware of his habits, so were always on the lookout for him.

One night, Bruadar told his family that he was going out to call on a particular neighbour and would return via the shortcut. The robbers, who were eavesdropping at the door, heard what he had said and hatched a plan to rob him on his way home.

They laid an ambush for him in a glen near to where he would cross. When they heard him coming, they rushed and attacked him, leaving him for dead when they had relieved him of the money he carried with him.

His family became worried when he did not return and went in search for him. To their utter dismay, they found his lifeless body slumped across the little humpback bridge that skirted along the base of the glen.

People who travelled through the glen and passed by the site of the murder of Bruadar would always remember the poor man who died an unnatural death at the hands of evil. They would say a prayer for his soul and throw a small stone onto the ground to show that he was remembered.

Gradually this practice caused a large memorial cairn of stones to be created, and the priest would say Mass here for poor Bruadar. Such cairns were known all across the land in the old tongue as *leacht*, and so this became known as *Leacht Bhruadair*, which was anglicised quite comically as Loughfouder.

THE MOVING BOG

A short distance north of Rathmore, near the border with County Cork, lies the small village of Gneeveguilla (Gníomh go Leith in Irish); the scene of a strange and tragic incident that occurred just after Christmas of 1896. This incident became known as 'the moving bog', but today it might be described less dramatically as a landslide. The disaster has been immortalised by the song of the same name, written by Donal Hickey.

On the night of 28 December, Con Donnelly, his wife Joanna, and five of his children went to bed as usual on a rather stormy and rainy night, unaware of the impending disaster that would strike them. Not far from the house (known as Quarry Lodge) was a large bog on the hillside owned by the Earl of Kenmare. Donnelly worked for the earl as a steward or, according to an Australian newspaper, as his quarry-man and bog ranger at another nearby quarry that was also in his ownership.

According to another newspaper, a boy passed by the house at midnight on his way home, but saw nothing untoward. At about four o'clock in the morning, local residents felt the earth shake and heard a low rumbling noise – but it was not until the morning that the devastation of the night's events were discovered. The bog, about a mile wide, half a mile long and 30 feet deep, had detached itself from the hillside in the night and slipped for some 2 miles down the valley, engulfing the Donnellys' cottage that lay directly in its path, as well as the outbuildings that contained their livestock. The huge river of bog had obliterated not just the cottage, but the Donnellys themselves as they slept, leaving no sign of the house or outbuildings but for the thatched roof that had been carried off some distance away. The only survivors of the tragedy were the family's dog and their 10-year-old daughter Katie, who had been staying at her grandmother's house, which she often did at Christmas time.

The confused dog was found the next day where the house should have been, along with a solitary cap belonging to one of the sons, but nothing else remained to show that the family had ever been there.

The quarry where Donnelly had worked was completely filled in and a bridge was destroyed, as was a powder magazine shed and much of the surrounding fields.

Within a week, all of the bodies of the Donnellys were found except one, which was discovered over a year later close to where the house had stood. Some of the cattle were found by the bridge at Annamore, where their bodies had become lodged. Another family in a nearby village, the Sullivans, had a lucky escape as, being awoken by the rumbling, they managed to flee from their house that became surrounded by peat.

Some forty-five families in all were affected by the moving bog, which eventually made its way into the River Flesk. Fields were covered, hay was destroyed along with livestock, and the salmon fishing was ruined, with many dead salmon found in and around the Flesk, which burst its banks due to the vast quantities of mud and peat. Some of the peat and mud reached as far as the Killarney lakes, with a bridge into the town becoming partially blocked.

Queen Victoria is said to have telegraphed Lord Kenmare for news of the disaster, and a fund was set up to provide relief to those who suffered. It was estimated that the cost to the county to remove the immense quantities of peat, to clear and repair the roads and, finally, to make good any other damage was up to £7,000.

In many cases it was nearly impossible, or too impractical, to clear the surrounding countryside of the dislodged peat. Locals simply waited for the good weather and gradually chipped away at the mess for turf to burn, which lasted up to four years for some.

According to a New South Wales newspaper, the disaster was not totally unexpected. Although several days of heavy rain were thought to be the immediate cause of the slide, local residents had feared something of this nature due to the build up of water over time. Water collected where the bog had been cut for turf, undermining the bog because no drainage channels had been made. People even noticed a trembling when walking on the unstable bog and some thought that the bog might be sitting on a subterranean lake.

Today, all surface evidence of the disaster is gone, but in December 1996, exactly 100 years after the disaster, a memorial was erected on the site of where the Donnelly house once stood.

St Fiachna and the Rolls of Butter

St Fiachna is the patron saint of the area of Bonane, a small townland not far south of Kenmare.

It is said that he was born near Kealkill in West Cork to an already large and struggling family. He was but one of three children born on the same day to the same poor exhausted woman, and the head of the household felt that they could not cope with one more child, never mind three!

He decided that the only option was to drown the poor babies, and so he left their fort the day after the birth and carried the three children in a basket to the nearby river for to throw them in, the poor mites. As he arrived on the bank of the river, he met a holy man kneeling in prayer by the water. He enquired as to the intentions of the man with the babies and, on discovering what he was going to do, the holy man took ownership of the children from him, saving their lives. He baptised them then and there in the river and knew they were destined to go on to great things. He was right, as all three children went on to become saints.

One May morning, while out walking near his church, Fiachna came across a shifty looking woman making butter, and hiding behind a tree while she did it.

'What has you making butter in this place?' asked Fiachna.

The young lady cursed at the saint and angrily told him to leave her alone and mind his own business.

'Why are you not making your butter at home?' he asked again, and again she cursed at him and told him to go away, although this time in more colourful language that cannot be printed here.

'I am merely concerned that you have no home in which to make your butter.'

The young lady then snapped and told him that she stole the milk from her neighbour's cow and is making the butter as quickly as she could before she was caught in the act.

'Now go away and bother me no more,' she retorted.

As with many Irish saints, Fiachna was not known for his patience.

'You have stolen milk on May morning of all mornings?' he shouted. 'Give the rolls of butter to me now!'

She began to realise the seriousness of her act and put the rolls of butter behind her back, just out of his reach. Fiachna became blind with rage at her insolence and struck her churn with his staff. At once the container turned to stone, as did her dasher and the rolls of butter she held in her hands. With the fright she threw them down and pulled her skirt up over her knees for to make a quick getaway.

Not being satisfied with simply petrifying the woman's utensils, Fiachna thought that he would make an example of her and a warning to all sinners. He pursued the poor woman relentlessly over the surrounding countryside, until she came to a river. Just as she was crossing it, he caught up with her and tapped her with his staff, petrifying her on the spot. Her wooden buckle fell off her clothes and onto the ground, taking root and growing into a bush.

The Rolls of Butter can be seen to this day in Bonane, as can the standing stone and bush – the remains of the poor woman – in nearby Gearhangoul.

The Gauger

In the old days a man lived on a mountain, where he kept a secret distillery for making poitín.

He had to smuggle the kegs of drink into the nearest town at opportune moments in order to sell them. On one particular day he sent his son to the town with the good stuff, but as his son was going down the road with the keg under his arm, he saw several men on horseback coming towards him and he knew that it was the Gauger and his men.

The son jumped over the ditch into a field to hide, but he took a nasty fall and let go of his keg. The poitín rolled away a good distance and kept going until it had rolled into some gorse bushes down at the bottom of the field. The young man decided to leave the keg where it lay, and as he got up he turned his coat inside out to change his appearance and came out of the field further up the road.

By this time the Gauger was coming very near to him. When he reached the distiller's son, he asked him if he had seen a young lad jump over the ditch with a keg under his arm and the boy said that he had not. The Gauger went inside the field to search and sure enough, after a while, he found the keg. He once again asked the boy if he had seen anybody go over the ditch and once more the boy said that he had not.

After some thought the Gauger said, 'Maybe it was yourself that went over the ditch!' and the boy admitted that it was him.

'Was it just now that you turned your coat?' asked the Gauger, to which the boy replied that it was. 'Now tell me what were you going to do with the keg?' asked the Gauger.

The boy pretended not to know who the Gauger was. 'My father gave it to me to present to the Gauger.'

The Gauger smiled and told him who he was. He gave the boy a key, and said, 'When you go to my house give it to the servant and tell her to put the keg into the cellar where she had put the one the evening before.'

The boy said he would do just that, but when he was about to start off, one of the men warned the Gauger that the young fellow was trying to make a fool of him.

The Gauger disagreed with his man, saying that the boy had an honest face, and sent him on his way with the keg in tow. When the boy came to the Gauger's house, he handed the key to the servant saying that he was told by the Gauger to take the keg of poítín that came in yesterday evening. She at once got it and gave it to him and the boy went off into town with a keg under each arm. The clever lad sold both kegs for a good price before returning back to his father with the money.

Later on, the Gauger invited a group of men to his house for the evening. After a good dinner, as they were sitting around the table, he asked one of his servants to bring up the two kegs from the cellar, brought in only yesterday and today.

'Well, sir,' she said, 'there's no keg from yesterday or today – didn't the boy you sent with the key of the cellar take it away to you, along with the one he was carrying?' At this the Gauger sat in stunned silence, for he knew he had been made a fool of by the quick-thinking lad. All of the men around the table laughed at the clever trick and so the Gauger shrugged his shoulders and laughed too.

'Well then,' he said, 'you may as well bring up the few bottles that are left and we'll drink to the young man's health!'

THE LIBERATOR AND THE GHOST

Daniel O'Connell, one of Ireland's most famous sons and known as 'The Liberator', features rather surprisingly in an old ghost story, related by Kerry schoolgirl Maria O'Rouke.

In the time when Daniel O'Connell was a barrister in Munster and before his campaigning for Catholic emancipation, an old woman came to him seeking his advice and wishing to tell her strange story to him. And so Daniel, not wishing to offend the woman, listened to her tale.

A few years earlier, a man she knew had come looking for a loan from her, knowing that she had saved a considerable sum. The man asked for IR£5, which was a small fortune in those times, promising that he would not need it for long and that she could ask for it back at any time. After some time had passed, the old lady had managed to get into debt and was sorely in need of the IR£5 that she had loaned – however, she was unable to get the money back as promised.

In desperation the old woman went to a crafty neighbour, hoping that he might be able to help recover the money with some clever trick or scheme, seeing that conventional methods had failed her. The neighbour left the old lady's house with a plan concocted, although he kept it to himself, carrying in his bag some strange black garb and a pair of horse's hooves. He brought them with him to the house of the man who had borrowed the IR£5. The crafty neighbour, knowing that the man took in lodgers, went to the house in the evening and requested a night's lodging.

He was given a room for the night and the people of the house retired to bed as usual. Very early in the morning the crafty neighbour got up and put on the hooves and began to gallop around the room with the noise terrifying everyone in the house, but no one was brave enough to investigate. Later on at midday, as no one had emerged from the room, the maid was reluctantly sent up to see if their guest was up – but when she heard the beating of hooves again she ran back down in fear to the man of the house.

Not so easily scared, the owner bounded up the stairs and burst into the room, impatient to be paid and rid of his lodger. To his terror, he saw a strange black figure with hooves prancing about the room, who he immediately took to be an evil ghost or even the devil himself.

Running back downstairs quickly, he sent for a priest to rid them of the terrifying apparition. When the priest arrived and climbed the stairs, the hoof noises began again and the apparition continued as the priest prayed and threw holy water around the place.

Returning down to the family without success, the priest asked if they had been cursed by anyone, committed a great sin or owed any kind of debt. It was at this point that the head of the house admitted that he borrowed IR£5 from an old woman, but had not paid it back as promised. The priest's eyes lit up, exclaiming that this deceit was surely the cause of their woes and that they must pay at once in order to be rid of their ghostly guest.

Listening at the door, the crafty neighbour heard the commotion as the family rushed about looking for the money in tins and draws to repay the old lady. With his bag packed he waited by the window until he saw the distressed borrower run out of the house with great haste to repay the old woman. Laughing to himself, he climbed out of the window, carefully shutting it behind him before he climbed down into the street and went home.

When the man returned, he and the priest timidly ventured up to the room to find it empty and the bed still made. The priest blessed the room with holy water, advising the man that they had had a lucky escape and always to pay his debts on time!

FACTION FIGHTING AT BALLYEIGH STRAND

Did you know that the innocent-looking blackthorn stick or shillelagh, used by many an old man to aid in their mobility, was originally a murderously efficient weapon used to cause harm during violent clashes between feuding groups in nineteenth-century Ireland?

Did you also know that the term 'to batter' (people, not fish) originated from the Irish term *batar*, which referred to the art of stick fighting?

Such battles were peculiar to this land and they spread fast from the time of their origins in Tipperary, 1805. The skirmishes became ruthlessly organised and efficient in the manner in which they pitted men and women against each other, sometimes to the death. Their battlegrounds were the fair greens, holy wells, markets, fairs, racecourses and even on the streets of towns and villages.

Anger was constantly simmering under the surface and it took little to tip groups over the edge. Many a minor disagreement would escalate quickly into a feud, and anything could set off a faction fight. Arguments over money, property, or simply drunken stupidity could have grave consequences.

Two North Kerry clans, the Cooleens and the Black Mulvihills/Lawlors, were well-established enemies in the nineteenth century. Their hatred of each other apparently stemmed from an incident one day at the Listowel Fair. A discussion arose as to which clan sold the superior quality of potato, probably nothing more than a case of bragging, slagging and male bravado. Testosterone took over and matters worsened with insults starting to be thrown, which were then replaced with sticks, stones and punches. The Black Mulvihills had to pack up and retreat due to their inferior numbers, but also given the fact that the Cooleens were local lads and had greater support from the townspeople.

The Black Mulvihills did not forget this embarrassment and a number of minor skirmishes followed at various locations afterwards, but the massive conflict that happened in 1834, on the feast of St John the Baptist, surpassed all others.

It was on this day that the fair and race meeting at Ballyheigue Strand was being held in honour of the saint, and it was said that well over 3,000 people attended. Stalls were erected on the sand in front of the Cashen schoolhouse and the day was the epitomy of gaiety, with exotic fruit, pig's feet, bannocks and breads of all shapes and sizes available to the hungry masses. Other tents sold ales, whiskies and poitín to refresh the weary traveller.

Matters took a turn for the worse around midday, when the Cooleens rowed over from the opposite side of the River Feale to Cashen for to challenge the Lawlors and Black Mulvihills to a fight. They thought that by attacking early in the day that they would have the advantage of surprise, but how wrong they were. They had blackthorns at the ready as they pulled their neamhógs up onto the strand to join some comrades already present.

The Cooleens charged at their opponents, but realised too late that there were 2,000 Lawlor and Black Mulvihill men and women waiting for them. They were hopelessly outnumbered and were beaten mercilessly. They knew that the only sensible option was to retreat, and this they did. They ran back to the boats and piled on, while others tried to swim across the estuary. The boats were overloaded and some capsized, while others sank outright. More had gathered on both sides of the river and threw stones, bottles and other missiles at the men struggling in the water. Those that decided to remain on the bank or made it to the other side were also beaten badly.

By the end of the day, some thirteen men had drowned, with another ten beaten to death. The real number may never be known, as others died some weeks and months afterwards from wounds sustained in the conflict.

Some believe that the English landlords of the time had engineered the feud in order to foster disunity among the locals. If this was the case, then they succeeded.

The dark cloud of bloodshed and shame hovered over the annual race meeting at Ballyeigh, and not long afterwards it was moved to Listowel, where it has been held every year to the present. Thankfully, faction fighting is a thing of the past and the Irish are not as angry as we apparently once were!

THE RIVALRY OF CLÍODHNA AND AOIBHEALL

Many Irish people will be familiar with tales of fairies and of banshees. Some may not realise that banshees are actually from the fairy realm, with the name originating from the Irish *Bean Sídhe* meaning fairy woman.

The banshee is a spirit who is said to forewarn of the death of a family member. She usually, but not always, only appears to the members of clans whose surnames contain the prefix Mac, or Ó. Some families even have particular banshees assigned to them. Some believe that banshees are the ghosts of young women who were brutally killed and died so horribly that their spirits are left to wander the world, watching their families and loved ones and warning them when a violent death is imminent.

Many years ago there were two sisters named Clíodhna and Aoibheall. Nothing unusual in that, you might think, but Clíodhna and Aoibheall were not usual – they were members of the fairy people. They were also both daughters of a powerful priest of the old ways, known only as the Red Druid. Clíodhna was queen of the fairies of south Munster and banshee of the Tuatha Dé Danann, while Aoibheall was queen of the fairies of north Munster and guardian of the Dál gCais.

Some stories may have you thinking that fairies were only interested in playing tricks on and scaring the living daylights out of the country people, and in this case it is somewhat true. From birth, the two girls had a competitive relationship with each other, and one getting the better over the other would result in some fierce jealousy and vindictive repercussions.

Given the rivalry that existed between them, they could not live together in the same place; but they did set aside their dis-trust of each other once a month when they met to play some tricks on the country people. The ladies each had their own palace hidden away within rocky clefts and outcrops in differ-ent parts of the country. Clíodhna lived at Carraig Chlíodhna,

near Mallow in County Cork, and Aoibheall lived at Carraig Liath, near Killaloe in County Clare. Both palaces were located in the territories of the peoples that they guarded.

Clíodhna had a ferocious appetite for young, handsome men, and it was not unheard of for her to leave her palace in disguise on fair days to pick up someone she fancied and bring them back to her palace. They, of course, would usually not be seen again.

One day Clíodhna had one of her itches, and so she went out into the wilds for to find a man to scratch it. She walked some distance and eventually came to the woods of Knockraha. She stepped in through the long curtains of ivy and over many fallen trees, when she came across some young men out stalking deer. She set her eyes on the strongest of them, a fine man with long red hair and dressed in the finest of threads. He wore a torc around his neck, signifying his high status, and a beautiful brooch clasp on his cloak. On seeing the visitor, the chieftain halted and alighted from his steed.

'I am The O'Keeffe. What is the reason you linger at this place?'

The fairy responded, 'I merely wish to spend some time with you, good sir. Might I be granted the honour of your company on this evening?'

The chieftain agreed and ordered his men to return to their encampment. Both he and Clíodhna spent the evening in the woods, drinking mead and making love. It was a long night of passion that seemed to be endless, but the morning did eventually come, and when O'Keeffe awoke he found himself alone in the woods, with nothing but the birds and the trees for company. His companion from the previous night had clearly abandoned him once her appetite for human flesh was satisfied.

The chieftain arose and got up on his horse to return to his fort. He was galloping through the humid woods when, all of a sudden, his horse halted with a jolt and reared up at the glowing spectacle of lady in a white robe, kneeling down and gathering mushrooms from the forest floor.

'I nearly killed you, be more careful, madam!' he said with shock in his voice. The young lady looked up and he felt a little lightheaded and something in his stomach started to spin.

'I am Aoibheall, and I do believe I love you,' said she.

O'Keeffe knew that what he felt in his stomach were butterflies, and he felt the love of a thousand hearts lay upon him.

'It is I that is in love with you, Lady Aoibheall.' He alighted from his steed and kneeled down beside Aoibheall and they spoke with each other for many hours until the sun began to set in the distance and the woods grew dim.

Clíodhna had left her palace in the rock and came looking for O'Keeffe for a second dose of chieftain, such was her appetite. She was surprised not to hear the men hunting, as he had told her was a daily occurrence here. She stepped in through woods and let out an ear-piercing scream of anger when she saw O'Keeffe and her sister deep asleep beside a fallen bough. Her expression of anger sent the birds scarpering for cover and shook the trees to their foundations, sending leaves everywhere.

The two lovers awoke and covered their ears for protection against the deafening cry.

O'Keeffe recognised Clíodhna and said, with a tremor in his voice, 'What is the matter, madam?'

'You are my conquest and you shall belong to no other!' she screamed. Both Aoibheall and O'Keeffe begged her to accept their union as one of true love and not for the mere satisfaction of the flesh. Full of jealously and bereft of mercy, Clíodhna shrieked that it was not to happen, took a rowan wand from her satchel and said some unintelligible words before striking her sister with it on the head. With a thud, Aoibheall fell to the ground and spun around and around in a whirlwind of whiteness, growing smaller all the time. When the motion stopped, a small white cat, a very beautiful cat, was left in its place.

Aoibheall ran back to her father, the Red Druid, and explained to him what her sister had done. He was appalled and tried all he could to change Aoibheall back to her normal self and break the charm, but he could not. His wicked daughter's spell was too powerful.

Clíodhna felt the pull of the keen coming on her and began to wail in grief for an unknown death. She did not understand why at the beginning, as she had not known of a member of the Tuath expected to die imminently, but it soon became clear to her when her own father fell to the ground in front of her, clutching his chest as he died of a broken heart with the words 'how could you do this?' on his lips.

Clíodhna wept uncontrollably at the realisation of the wickedness of her acts, for the loss of her sister and father. Her wails of grief could be heard far across Munster, and it is said to have been the only time a banshee cried *after* the death of someone.

The spectre of a white cat still wanders the woods of Knockraha, and it is said that this is Aoibheall searching for a spell to break the charm so that she can be reunited with her true love.

7

THINGS RELIGIOUS
AND IRRELIGIOUS

LISLAUGHTIN ABBEY AND GLEANN CLUASACH

The Franciscan Friary at Lislaughtin is located one mile to the north of Ballylongford. It was built in 1470 by the O'Connors of Carrigafoyle and was a place of spiritual refuge for just over 100 years, continuing even after Henry VIII passed laws dissolving all religious houses.

These days the building is nothing more than an impressive ruin and graveyard, but in days past it was a centre of learning and worship of some repute, with a large complex for the friars and settlements that grew up all around it.

In the year 1580, a very sad incident took place at Lislaughtin, one that reverberates to this day in the area. A battalion of British Crown soldiers was on manoeuvre in the locality when they marched past the abbey, which was supposed to be vacated following the king's orders decades ago. They heard a bell ring from inside the church. It was the call to prayer, but the commanding officer thought that it was an act of mockery and so, flying into a rage, gave the order to charge.

The monks fled in terror and ran in all directions across the neighbouring countryside in order to save themselves from certain death. The majority escaped successfully, but three older monks by the names of Fr Hanrahan, Fr O'Shea, and Fr Scanlon were not able to move as quickly as some of their more spritely brethren.

They were able to get as far as a small valley near Tarbert before the soldiers caught up with them. The soldiers bound their hands together and strapped them to the rear of their horses.

With blind rage in their eyes the soldiers screamed at them, 'We'll make sure you hear no more papist bells in your time!' and with that they took out knives and sliced the ears from the poor men's heads. The valley forever after became known as Gleann Cluasach, or Valley of Hearing.

As if this act were not enough, the men were dragged back to the abbey and taken in front of the high altar, where they were mercilessly bludgeoned to death before having their heads severed from their bodies.

It is said that the screams of the poor monks can be heard on the anniversary of their slaying every year.

SOUPERS, JUMPERS AND PERVERTS

It really is difficult to record any folklore from any part of Ireland without touching on the dark days of the famine time and time again. This is particularly true of the areas on the western fringes of the island, such as Kerry.

So many men, women and children were just left to starve on the roadsides or in the ditches by an uncaring caretaker government. The demise of the wretched masses was hastened by the continued exportation by England of other foodstuffs from the beleaguered nation, turning many parts of the island into desolate wastelands.

Many in the British Church believed that the Great Hunger was a punishment visited on the Irish by God for their lazy ways. Many landlords and agents of the Church were guilty of partaking in the exploitation of the general desperation that the poor felt during those horrible years, and took the opportunity to either evict helpless tenants, try to convert them to Protestantism, or both.

A brainwave came over a certain Anglican Reverend by the name of Dallas, from Hampshire, who set up the 'Irish Church

Missions to the Roman Catholics'. Its aim was to educate the Irish in the evil ways of Roman Catholicism, and he believed that by dealing with the Irish through the medium of their native language that they may give up the folly that was their obsession with Popery.

Missionary centres were set up in many places throughout the island, but particularly in Dublin, Conamara and Kerry. One specific centre was Lough House, just south of Dingle, and the missionaries would go out every morning and travel from cabin to cabin throughout the peninsula to minister to the locals. They would agree to provide soup on the strict condition that the poor people convert to Protestantism, in what could only be described as a form of blackmail. Servants of God, indeed!

Elena Danaan

Many Irish did convert out of desperation, in an attempt to save themselves and their families from certain starvation, but what usually followed was their ostracisation by their own communities, who branded them with derogatory terms such as soupers or perverts: terms which refer to their acceptance of nourishment or for converting to a false religious belief.

In typical Irish style, many also turned this situation around to their advantage and became known as 'soupers and jumpers'.

These were people who converted to Protestantism for a bowl of soup and then jumped back to Catholicism once they had it past their lips!

One observer of the missions in 1828 described this practice in excellent form:

> *The converts are like birds, which visit milder climates at intervals – but their coming is a proof of great severity in their native country, and they return when the iron days are passed, and the sun cheers them from home.*

Sack 'em Ups!

The secret exhumation of deceased persons from graves was a fairly common occurrence in Ireland, and elsewhere, some 200 years ago. Before the Anatomy Act of 1832, the only supply of fresh corpses to the medical schools for the purpose of anatomy and dissection came from those condemned to death for crimes committed, or else those who died in the workhouses and whose bodies were not claimed by any family.

The availability of bodies for this purpose was not nearly sufficient for the demands of the medical students or lecturers, and so a black market quickly developed for the acquisition of corpses. The fresher the corpse, the higher the price paid.

As there was good money to be made in bodysnatching, there was no shortage of people willing to put their souls at risk of eternal damnation in order to do the most grisly of tasks. These people became known as 'Sack 'em Ups' or 'Resurrectionists' and were despised by all levels of society, except for the respected profession that hired them. This practice of bodysnatching was of course illegal, and many graveyards erected towers and employed armed guards to protect the recently deceased against such a crime.

It was a long time ago that Midge O'Sullivan, from the village of Sneem, died of the consumption; an ailment we thankfully don't see much of these days. Stricken with grief, his family wanted to give him the finest of send-offs, and so a grand three-day wake was held, followed by the most honourable of funerals.

He was laid to rest in the family vault in the local burial ground, where his mother and father had been laid to rest before him. Given the risk of bodysnatching, his family took turns in guarding the vault night after night. The usual timeframe would be one month from the time of death, when the medical colleges would lose interest due to decomposition.

For a couple of nights, Midge's family kept watch at the entrance to the vault. On the third night his brother was on guard, but he was a little worse for wear from the drink and it was not long before he was asleep on the job.

Can you guess what happened next? Well, just before sunrise, two lads rode up to the burial ground on horses. A favourite trick of the Sack 'em Ups was to cover the hooves of their horses with socks, so as to muffle their sounds and prevent drawing any attention to their illicit night-time activity in the burial ground. They crept in the gate and saw the drunk asleep beside the vault. To see if they would disturb him, they gave him a little nudge and then a larger nudge, but he made no movement whatsoever apart from a garbled snore, so they knew that they were okay to continue with their work.

They wedged their crowbars under the large granite slab that blocked the entrance to the vault and moved it to one side, looking down inside.

'We hit the jackpot, boy!' said the first man, and with that slid down into the vault. They were about to prepare the corpse for removal, when they heard a priest and a number of men enter the graveyard. The second man quickly gathered up their equipment and jumped down into the vault, hiding

behind a couple of the older coffins, hoping the men would leave soon.

'What are ye doing, you amadán?' said the priest to the drunk, and gave him such a clatter as to awaken him with a violent jolt. 'And here you are asleep with the vault left open beside you, so anybody could come and go while you slept!'

The man was too drunk to speak, or even to remember that it was not open when he'd arrived, and so the men discussed among themselves the carelessness of the undertakers to have left the vault open after the funeral. They grabbed ahold of the slab and lifted it back up over the entrance to the vault, not knowing about the two living men that hid within.

The Sack 'em Ups felt around in the darkness until they reached the entrance slab, thinking a firm shove would shift it, but they were wrong. They pushed and pushed, but could not budge it even an inch. As the panic set in on them, they started to scream and holler for anybody to help them.

Nobody heard.

As the air within their prison slowly turned bad, they continued to scratch at the slab until their fingers were bloodied and their spirits broken. They barely lasted one night in the vault until they too expired.

It was not until the next family funeral, two years later, that their shrivelled remains were discovered and the family realised what had happened. The bodies were removed from the vault and from consecrated ground, and were buried outside the church walls as convicts.

Other titles by the authors:

Gary Branigan:
Ancient and Holy Wells of Dublin
Fountains of Dublin
Cavan Folk Tales

Luke Eastwood:
The Druid's Primer
The Journey
Through the Cracks in the Concrete the Wilderness Grows

Ireland is famed throughout the world for the art of storytelling. The seancaithe and scéalaí, the tradition bearers and storytellers passed the old stories down through the generations. Today, in the 21st century, there has been a revivial od the ancient art founded in 2003, Storytellers of Ireland / Aos Scéal Éireann is an all-Ireland voluntary organisation with charitable status.

Our aim is to promote the practice, study and knowledge of oral storytelling in Ireland through the preservation and perpetuation of traditional storytelling and the development of storytelling as a contemporary art. We aim to foster storytelling skills among all age groups, from all cultural backgrounds. We also aim to explore new contexts for storytelling in public places – in schools, community centres and libraries, in care centres and prisons, in theatres, arts centres and at festivals throughout the entire island of Ireland.

Storytelling is an intimate and interactive art. A storyteller tells from memory rather than reading from a book. A tale is not just the spoken equivalent of a literary short story. It has no set text, but is endlessly re-created in the telling. The listener is an essential part of the storytelling process. For stories to live, they need the hearts, minds and ears of listeners. Without the listener there is no story.

Le fiche bliain anuas, tá borradh agus fás tagaithe ar sheanghairm inste scéal. Tá clú agus cáil ar na scéalta ársa agus ar an seanchas atá le fáil i nÉirinn. Le déanaí tá siad arís i mbéal an phobail, idir óg is sean, is i ngach áird is aicme.